Flexible and Virtual Working

Steve Shipside

- Fast track route to getting the most out of being a remote worker

- Covers all the key aspects of flexible and virtual working, from teleworking and telecommuting to groupware and virtual call centres

- Lessons and tips from some of the world's great remote work successes, such as AT&T and Lasair, and ideas from the smartest thinkers, including Alvin Toffler and Gil Gordon

- Includes a glossary of key concepts and a comprehensive resources guide

essential management thinking at your fingertips

LIFE & WORK

10.05

The right of Steve Shipside to be identified as the author of this work has been asserted in accordance with the Copyright, Designs and Patents Act 1988

First published 2002 by
Capstone Publishing (a Wiley company)
8 Newtec Place
Magdalen Road
Oxford OX4 1RE
United Kingdom
http://www.capstoneideas.com

CIP catalogue records for this book are available from the British Library and the US Library of Congress

ISBN 1-84112-200-9

This book is printed on acid-free paper

Substantial discounts on bulk quantities of Capstone books are available to corporations, professional associations and other organizations. Please contact Capstone for more details on +44 (0)1865 798 623 or (fax) +44 (0)1865 240 941 or (e-mail) info@wiley-capstone.co.uk

Contents

Introduction to ExpressExec

ExpressExec is 3 million words of the latest management thinking compiled into 10 modules. Each module contains 10 individual titles forming a comprehensive resource of current business practice written by leading practitioners in their field. From brand management to balanced scorecard, ExpressExec enables you to grasp the key concepts behind each subject and implement the theory immediately. Each of the 100 titles is available in print and electronic formats.

Through the ExpressExec.com Website you will discover that you can access the complete resource in a number of ways:

» printed books or e-books;
» e-content – PDF or XML (for licensed syndication) adding value to an intranet or Internet site;
» a corporate e-learning/knowledge management solution providing a cost-effective platform for developing skills and sharing knowledge within an organization;
» bespoke delivery – tailored solutions to solve your need.

Why not visit www.expressexec.com and register for free key management briefings, a monthly newsletter and interactive skills checklists. Share your ideas about ExpressExec and your thoughts about business today.

Please contact elound@wiley-capstone.co.uk for more information.

Introduction to Expression

Introduction to Flexible and Virtual Working

Remote working, teleworking, and telecommuting are re-shaping the way we work, the way we manage others, and the understanding of what companies and jobs are now and how they will be in the future.

"The single most anti-productive thing we can do is ship millions of workers back and forth across the landscape every morning and evening."

Alvin Toffler, Future Shock

Remote working, which is the literal meaning of teleworking (see Chapter 2), is one of the most significant shifts in the landscape of the working world. The International Telework Association & Council (ITAC) calculates that by 2004 30 million people in the US, and a similar number in the EU, will be working remotely at least one day a week. ITAC's calculations suggest that beyond that date the number of teleworkers in the EU may accelerate to outpace the US, and reach the total of 40 million by 2007. The growth is explosive, the question is: why?

There is a stereotype of remote working, and in particular home-working, that suggests the principal benefits are flexibility and freedom from supervision enjoyed by the individuals. In part this is true. There is no doubt that telework converts do enjoy a feeling of liberty, and that this has an important part to play in shifting attitudes towards the balance of work and family life in the new millennium. Important as that is, individual freedom remains just a small part of the picture, and the benefits to companies, national economies, and the environment are often overlooked.

Productivity studies suggest that remote workers may be up to 25% more productive than their office-bound counterparts. Absenteeism is reduced, real estate costs fall, and staff retention can be helped by flexible schemes. So much so, in fact, that a number of studies suggest that a company can save over $11,000 (almost £7000) per remote worker per year – even including the cost of paying for all the technology (see Chapter 7 for details).

Remote working offers new hope for rural regeneration and remote communities. It can make the most of time zones and language differences (see Chapter 5) and it can reduce congestion and pollution, which itself can improve the company's bottom line. It is no accident that a number of the better-known schemes in the US were introduced after the advent of clean air legislation (and with it the threat of taxation or fines for bad practice) in certain states.

Remote working pioneers like AT&T report that the inclusion of teleworking in job profiles gives them the edge in recruitment, and as the Web becomes ever more pervasive in developed countries so the technology barriers to telework disappear. The introduction of high-bandwidth communication to the home, and high-speed, always-on mobile telephony are likely to continue the trend towards permanent connectivity, and with it the options for remote collaboration.

Which is not to say that teleworking is right for everyone, or that those who can telework should do so all the time. But it does mean that companies would be rash not to consider what teleworking can do for them and for their workforce. Or as Garry Mathiason, a partner at the law firm of Littler, Mendelson, Fastiff, Tichy & Mathiason puts it on the City of Boulder telework Website: "Telecommuting is the way we're going to work. If you don't include telecommuting in your program, your company will not be competitive."

What is Flexible and Virtual Working?

Including a study of Jack Nilles, the "father of telecommuting," definitions of "teleworking" and "telecommuting," a look at five different kinds of remote working, a consideration of remote working as a means of tapping into a talent pool no matter how far-flung the individuals may be, and a look at how remote working can benefit the environment.

Before attempting to define some of the terminology used in flexible and virtual working, it is worthwhile taking a brief look at the man who, to many, is seen as having pioneered that concept – Jack Nilles.

JACK NILLES – "THE FATHER OF TELECOMMUTING"

Jack Nilles, dubbed the "father of telecommuting," headed-up the preliminary design-states of space vehicles and communications systems for the Aerospace Corporation in Los Angeles, the US Air Force's "space engineering think-tank" which advised NASA. His role was twofold: helping NASA select the survey equipment for locating the landing sites for the Apollo moon-landings, and consulting with NASA on weather and earth resource satellites; and leading a team that developed fore-casts in 1970–1 for Jim Fletcher, the then incoming director of NASA, for the civilian use of space in the 1980s. Nilles was also a consultant to the Science Advisory Council for Presidents Kennedy and Johnson.

At the time of the first moon-landings, the idea of a personal computer in every home was not even a glimmer in a computer marketer's eye, yet the potential for remote connection by telephone had already been demonstrated, and Nilles' work had always emphasized the culture, rather than the technology, required for teleworking to take place. Nilles says:

> "Strangely enough, I was teleworking in the mid-1960s, since our Air Force colleagues on our joint 'campus' had an encrypted, private, closed-circuit TV link with the Pentagon. Because it was so expensive it was used only for very important meetings. So I had to spend a lot of time 'commuting' between Los Angeles and Washington, DC. On one occasion, about 1965 or so, I flew all night to DC for a one-hour meeting with the Under-secretary of the Air Force; the meeting was cancelled and I got back on a plane to LA that afternoon, thinking: 'This is ridiculous! I could have accomplished the objectives of the meeting without ever leaving LA, given the right technology.'"
>
> "Late in 1970 (or early 1971) I was trying to see how all this sophisticated defense technology could be used in the 'real world.' On one occasion I met a regional planner who asked

me: 'Why, if you could put man on the moon, can't you do something about traffic? Why can't you get people to work at home?' At that point everything clicked for me. Why not indeed? I began to analyze the situation from first principles: why do we have traffic? - half of it is people driving to work; what do they do when they get to work? - half of them sit at desks phoning someone somewhere else; why do they have to drive somewhere to do that? - because that's the way we've 'always' done it. Well, to shorten the story, I decided to try out this idea of trading telecommunications for transportation in a real-world situation (to do it I had to quit my job at Aerospace and invent a new one at the University of Southern California). It worked! However, 'the telecommunications–transportation trade-off' was not a catchy name for this, so I decided to call it 'telecommuting,' a form of 'telework,' in 1973. The rest is . . . "

It was during his time as Director for Interdisciplinary Research at the University of Southern California, the post he mentions above, that Nilles began his formal research on telecommuting and teleworking.

DEFINITIONS OF TELEWORKING AND TELECOMMUTING

Flexible working, remote working, virtual offices, virtual working, alternative officing, alternative work styles, long-distance working, alternative workplacing, virtual workplacing, telecommuting and tele-working, are all terms used to describe working patterns where the work is moved to the workers and not *vice versa*. They often overlap and are sometimes synonymous but for the purpose of definition the first word has to go to Jack Nilles:

"Teleworking, telecommuting, what's the difference? Here are my definitions (since I coined the two terms in 1973, I get some priority to decide):"
"Teleworking: any form of substitution of information technologies (such as telecommunications and computers) for work-related travel."

"Telecommuting: moving the work to the workers instead of moving the workers to work; periodic work out of the principal office, one or more days per week either at home or in a telework center. The emphasis here is on reduction or elimination of the daily commute to and from the workplace."

"Telecommuting is a form of teleworking; all telecommuters are teleworkers but not all teleworkers are telecommuters. We concentrated on telecommuting in the early years of our research because that was where all the leverage was: getting people out of their cars during rush hours. Also, in my definition, telecommuters are generally employees of some organization, as contrasted to people with home-based businesses. Again, the distinction is that, absent telecommuting, these people would be going to a workplace somewhere else."

"The term teleworking, on the other hand, includes such variations as home-based businesses that use telecommunications to work with their customers, as well as those who may commute every day to some traditional location but use information technologies to deal mostly with people in other cities, states, or countries. The number of teleworkers in the world is also growing, possibly even at a faster rate than the number of telecommuters. The immense growth of the Internet, assuming that it survives the expansion problems, is a major factor in this."

"Finally, teleworking is the preferred term in Europe where, until recently, there was no accepted word for commuting. So, in Europe we have télétravail, Telearbeit, telelavoro, teletrabajo, and telearbet (telework in French, German, Italian, Spanish, and Swedish, respectively), but only télépendulaire, Telependlung and telependla (telecommuting in French, German, and Swedish) as far as I know."

To which teleworking consultant Gil Gordon adds that:

". . . in my opinion, the difference is minimal. The term 'telework' tends to be used more in Europe and some other countries, while 'telecommuting' is used more in the US. Some people prefer the word 'telework' because it's a more accurate description of the concept – the 'tele' prefix means 'distance,' so 'telework' means 'work at a distance.' The telework advocates also believe that 'telecommuting' has too strong a connotation about the commuting aspect, and that 'telework' is a broader and more inclusive term ... Whatever you choose to call it, the underlying concept is the same: decentralizing the office, and using different ways of bringing the work to the workers. It doesn't make much difference (to me, at least) what you call it – as long as you do it."

Gil Gordon (www.gilgordon.com)

Ursula Huws, associate fellow of the Institute for Employment Studies in the UK, breaks teleworking into five major activities:

» multi-site teleworking – an employee alternates between working on the employer's premises and working elsewhere;
» tele-homeworking – work is based exclusively in the home and carried out for a single employer;
» freelance teleworking – working for a variety of employers;
» mobile teleworking – typically working "on-the-road" using portable/mobile equipment; and
» relocated back-office functions.

Whilst being able to complete the work away from the office is a key part of teleworking, there's a great deal more to it than taking home a couple of files to work on. The key element of teleworking is the decentralization of the workplace, not the technology it involves, and even in this day and age it may still require nothing more technically complex than a pen, pad, and telephone. There's no denying, however, that technology has meant enormous advances in teleworking and in our understanding of it. Portable computers, the spread of Internet access, and mobile communications mean that it is possible for a worker on the move to link up to their company network as they globetrot. Video-conferencing allows for "face-to-face" meetings between people who have never actually met. Whiteboarding technology means that two remote workers can be looking at and correcting the same spreadsheet, or computer-aided design, at the same time. Virtual Private Networks mean that workers in Dubai, Darwin, Detroit, and Doncaster can all be hooked up securely to their company system as if they were sitting at their desks in the office – and all for the cost of a local call.

Remote working has significant implications for the way companies work. As corporations become increasingly far-reaching and markets become global, it is often the case that the best project manager, or adviser, or colleague is no longer down the hall but in the next county, country, or continent.

> "Telework is much more than a cyber-hula-hoop. The reason it is expanding the way it is derives from the fact that it appears to benefit all concerned: employers, teleworkers, and the communities in which they live. Increasing global competition, coupled with the toppling of telecommunications regulatory barriers, is producing more awareness that many forms of work are independent of the locations of either the worker or the employer. As the costs of transport (read telecommunications) become small relative to the cost of labor, then there is a great incentive/temptation to look beyond one's own back yard for the necessary expertise."
>
> *Jack Nilles*

Remote working means the opportunity to include individuals and their skills who would otherwise have been excluded from companies and projects simply because they didn't work in the same building. It even goes beyond that and makes it possible to create new teams to take on projects in a way that simply cannot be done in conventional work practice.

In the run-up to the year 2000, western businesses worked furiously to clear their systems of any Y2K bugs. Shortness of time and a shortage of skills meant that it became increasingly common for programmers in the US to hand over their work at the end of their working day to partner programmers in India who were just starting their working day (see Chapter 5, The Global Dimension). In the same way, it is an established practice for American doctors who dictate patient notes all day to send their recordings to the Indian subcontinent in the evening where they are transcribed and returned ready for start of work the next day. Films being shot in Hollywood can send their digital rushes by cable to the UK where the digital special effects houses of Soho can create effects and edit the film before returning it by the next morning.

That kind of remote collaboration expands the available workforce and the limits of the working day.

Remote working can also mean enormous productivity gains and cost savings. Teleworking can mean a new lease of working life for disabled workers faced with access problems at the office. It can greatly reduce real estate costs for companies, and allow them to benefit from more cost-effective satellite or shared offices. It can provide enormous flexibility by making better use of part-time workers. For example, the idea of the virtual call-center where operators, instead of coming to work in a single call-center, log on to the exchange from their homes, at which point they can receive and deal with calls coming into the center exactly as if they were there in person.

It can provide a crucial means of retaining key staff in circumstances where they would otherwise be lost, such as maternity or family moves away from the city. Nick Shelness – chief technical officer for Lotus in the US – lives in Scotland and works from a remote mill (see Chapter 5). As such it offers a potential solution to the issues of gridlock, congestion, and urban blight. In fact, as we saw above, it was the issue of traffic that prompted Nilles to start his research into telework in the first place.

Last but most certainly not least, teleworking provides a glimmer of hope for a society where energy and pollution problems are reaching a crisis point.

"If 10% of the nation's workforce telecommuted one day a week, we would avoid the frustration of driving 24.4 million miles, we'd breathe air with 12,963 tons less air pollution, and we'd conserve more than 1.2 million gallons of fuel each week."

Carol Browner, Environmental Protection Agency
Administrator

KEY LEARNING POINTS

» Although "telework" and "telecommute" are often used interchangeably, the nature of remote work covers a number of different approaches.
» Through its flexibility it enables different patterns of work and different types of collaboration. It can call on skills and

The Evolution of Flexible and Virtual Working

Starting with the invention of the telephone and its impact on remote working, and moving through to the coming of age of remote working with the advent of the personal computer and the subsequent explosive growth in telework, this chapter continues with a look at the rise of remote working outside of the US, its birthplace, and considers how the European model may well outstrip the US, while the Japanese approach looks set to lag. The chapter concludes with a time-line of major events.

THE INVENTION OF THE TELEPHONE AND ITS IMPACT ON REMOTE WORKING

Although we now associate teleworking with the advent of the home or portable computer, it is wrong to think that teleworking was born of the PC era (the 1980s). In fact, its beginnings can reasonably be traced back a hundred years before the PC appeared on a desktop, since telecommuting first started with the advent of the telephone. One story has it that the first telecommuter was a bank president who had a telephone link from his Boston office to his home in Somerville, Massachusetts in 1877, although telework could be claimed to have started the year before according to Herbert N. Casson's *History of the Telephone* (www.bookrags.com/books/thott/PART1.htm). Casson relates a demonstration by Watson, the assistant of Alexander Graham Bell, who gave a lecture by telephone from Salem to Boston. Most importantly of all, the lecture was sent by telephone to the *Boston Globe* which announced that "this special despatch of the *Globe* has been transmitted by telephone in the presence of twenty people, who have thus been witnesses to a feat never before attempted – the sending of news over the space of sixteen miles by the human voice."

Newspapers were to be one of the first industries to understand the importance of the phone. By having a copy-taker at one end to write down what they heard, and a reporter acting as eyewitness at the other, the newspapers had created their own breed of remote worker – a worker, in fact, whose singular value was that he was somewhere else. Whilst the advent of word processors, faxes, and modems has now largely sent the copy-taker the way of the dodo, remote correspondents were to telework that way for over a century.

The telephone, fax, and telegram have long enabled satellite offices and travelling sales staff to keep in touch with their headquarters and keep the organization going. The step, however, that most dramatically changed the working landscape was to come with the advent of computers.

THE ADVENT OF THE PERSONAL COMPUTER

Telework consultant Gil Gordon tells of computer-based telework going back to the 1960s: "I have heard stories of companies that had employees working at home doing a job that has been mostly forgotten by today's workforce. They were using IBM keypunch machines to produce those old-fashioned data-entry cards that were used before magnetic tape or diskettes."

While computer-based telework pre-dates the home computer, it was nonetheless the invention of early personal computers in the 1970s (it was in 1973 that Jack Nilles coined the terms "telecommute" and "telework"), and more particularly the IBM PC in 1981, that meant that computers became popular in business, and then in the mid-1980s the advent of laptops meant they could be moved more easily and they started to appear in homes. It soon became clear that it was possible for a home-based computer, a computer on the desk in an office or remote branch, and even a laptop on the move, to run the same programs. Modem access, once the preserve of academia and science, became increasingly popular with the opening up of the Internet to commercial companies, the first of which, MCI, started offering its commercial e-mail service in 1988. By the mid-1990s, with the Web now a fully-fledged commercial entity and competition amongst ISPs to offer ever-cheaper access packages to the home, the barriers to remote working were tumbling down and the number of teleworkers was ramping up.

THE EXPLOSIVE GROWTH IN TELEWORK

Jack Nilles tells the story of its growth as being one that follows a logistic or epidemic curve. "This is an S-shaped curve that starts with fairly small annual growth, then grows approximately exponentially for a while, then begins to slow down, and finally nears some maximum value, beyond which it will grow no further. This later part happens when all the live teleworkers who are ever going to telework are doing it."

There are no reliable statistics for the early days, although Nilles has his own estimates. "In 1970, when I first started looking into what we now call telecommuting, we had maybe a couple of thousand telecommuters. By 1980, there were about 100,000 telecommuters in the US, according to my forecasts (no one was actually asking such survey questions at the time). In 1990 the number had risen to about 2.4 million, according to my forecasts, and about 3.4 million, according to Tom Miller's [of New York research consultancy FIND/SVP] surveys of US households.''

Nilles forecasted 7.8 million teleworkers by 1994, FIND/SVP gave a figure of 9.1 million, rising to over 13 million in 1997. Nilles' forecasts meant that the US alone would have 24.7 million teleworkers by the year 2000.

In October 2000 ITAC announced that over 2.8 million new teleworkers had joined the ranks of the remote workforce in the US in a study which came up with the figure of 23.6 million teleworkers nationwide. The figure didn't correlate exactly with Nilles, but it was close, and ITAC continues to use Nilles' forecasting model to estimate future growth, concluding that there would be as many as 30 million teleworkers by the end of 2004, and 40 million by the end of 2010.

About which Nilles himself comments: ''All of this is not inevitable, of course. It's just that, if you believe that history can teach us anything, then there is a reasonable chance that one of five Americans will be telecommuting in five years. By the way, those numbers relate just to telecommuting. They exclude other forms of teleworking, including the many home-based businesses involved in teleworking.''

In other words, one in five of the American workforce will be doing their company work from home; that's not including those whose home is their company's base. As impressive as that figure is, the growth of teleworking in the US may yet be overshadowed by developments elsewhere.

THE RISE OF EUROPEAN REMOTE WORKING

While telework is seen as something of an American phenomenon, the growth of remote working in Europe looks set to outstrip it in terms of absolute numbers, and in some countries it is already way ahead in terms of *per capita* percentages. The European countries that have taken the lead in terms of mobile telephony and high-speed data transfer to the home have also, perhaps unsurprisingly, become those where teleworking is most prevalent. ITAC points to a 1999 survey in western Europe that shows Finland to be ahead of the world in terms of the percentage of people working remotely, with 10.8% of the workforce teleworking. Finland was followed by the Netherlands with

8.3% and Sweden with 8%. By comparison, the US figure at that point was 6.8%.

Nilles comments that: "I have spent considerable time over the past five years looking into teleworking around the rest of the world. I estimate that the US is five to ten years ahead of most other countries, except perhaps the UK, in the development of teleworking. Most of the action is in Europe, where the European Commission and France Telecom have been very active in promoting teleworking. There is also some teleworking going on in Asia, particularly India and the Philippines. But the growth rates in the rest of the world may be higher than those in the US so the balance of teleworkers could change significantly in the next two decades."

In fact, according to ITAC the EU countries also look set to hit the figure of 30 million teleworkers by the end of 2004, and could go on to arrive at 40 million in 2007 – some three years ahead of the US.

The EU agrees. In 1999 the EU-sponsored Electronic Commerce and Telework Trends Survey found that:

> "Germany has been faced with a telework boom, experiencing enormous telework growth rates over the past five years. Almost all large organizations are already practising telework, the smaller ones are following along the same routes. Despite this growth rate, Germany is still not the country leading in terms of telework penetration: Finland, the Netherlands, Sweden, Denmark and the UK all reach even higher penetration rates up to almost 11% of the workforce in Finland as opposed to 4.5% in Germany."

> "Given the fact that, on average, 60% of the workforce and more than 30% of decision-makers in establishments in Europe express an interest in telework or already practise telework it can be assumed that there is a large potential for a further (and even more rapid) uptake of telework in the coming years. These figures do not include mobile teleworkers and supplementary teleworkers. Bearing this in mind the potential will be even higher."

By this point a number of facilitating technologies are in place. Internet access is a worldwide phenomenon and broadband is becoming common in the more developed countries. In the US and some European countries, such as the Netherlands, cable has become established as a means of megabit access speeds, which in turn have brought the possibility of high-speed data transfer and cheap videoconferencing to the home. Elsewhere in Europe, Digital Subscriber Line (DSL) technologies have been installed. DSL allows megabit access speeds over conventional phone lines without disrupting the normal voice traffic. Virtual Private Networks (VPNs) mean that a worker based anywhere in the world can connect to the Net using a local ISP (and thus paying local rates) and from there be hooked up over a secure connection to the office network exactly as if he or she was in the office building itself.

At the same time the growth of Personal Digital Assistants (PDAs) means that being a remote worker no longer means even having a full-blown computer. Wireless communications and synchronizing software mean that a hand-held device, small enough to fit in a shirt pocket, may be all that is needed for a worker not only to stay in e-mail contact, but also to input directly to the spreadsheets and groupware of the corporation.

Taking into account all the different forms of remote working – be they telecommuting, taking work home, or keeping in touch on the move – the question becomes less "who is teleworking?" and more an issue of "who *isn't*?"

Yet there remains a significant difference between using technology to hook up remotely while on the move, or for one day a week's telecommuting, and taking the step of opting to move out of the office altogether. Telecommuting's arguments in terms of productivity, cost-savings, flexibility, and even ecological awareness, are undeniable, yet that doesn't mean the practice is suitable for all, or free from downsides.

As telework becomes more commonplace, so the debates as to its downsides become more common. In particular there are management issues in which companies fear that they lose control of their workforce, and individual managers, whose charges are now physically removed from them, can feel that their role is undermined. Workers can feel estranged from the company, not least since working from home still doesn't have the status of office work, and is sometimes not taken seriously by colleagues. On a social level there is the problem of a feeling of missing out; what teleworking evangelist June Langhoff describes as "water-cooler withdrawal." Furthermore, there is the suspicion that many senior managers accept teleworking for the cost benefits, but see those who telework as less committed to the company, and thus the first to be "let go" when times turn bad.

THE JAPANESE QUESTION

It remains significant that for all the association of technology with telecommuting, there is at least one very clear reminder that acceptance of the one does not translate to the other. Wendy Spinks of the Science University of Tokyo concludes that:

> "Contrary to popular wisdom, Japan is neither at the forefront of ICT penetration nor cutting-edge applications thereof. In fact the Japanese business environment is characterised by considerable conservatism in its approach to both e-business and work arrangements."

> "The EU-sponsored Electronic Commerce and Telework Trends survey's best assessment of the number of teleworkers in Japan was based on a 1996 figure which set the number of teleworkers as a mere 1.5 per cent of the workforce. That survey is still the last one referred to by the Japanese Organization of Teleworkers, although they do expect the figure to rise to nearly 2.5 million workers by the end of 2001. Even so that is a remarkably low figure, which the survey explains as being cultural."

> "Traditional Japanese corporate culture and traditional business practices are often cited as barriers to achieving stated telework objectives. The deep-rooted emphasis on face-to-face communication and poor evaluation skills of managers are two factors singled out specifically. Lack of manager awareness of telework and a preference for hierarchical management systems are additional factors. A lack of clear-cut missions and/or job descriptions is a further constraint. Elsewhere, a lack of awareness of the potential for micro outsourcing in Japanese corporate circles is seen as another hurdle."

The example of Japan makes it clear that, while the development and increasing availability of technology may help the spread of remote working, it is clear that the take-up of teleworking now and in the future has a great deal more to do with social and corporate culture than with bits and bytes.

TIME-LINE

» **1876–7**: Alexander Graham Bell demonstrates that his invention, the telephone, can be used to transmit a lecture from Salem to Boston, where it is printed by a newspaper. A bank manager is reputed to become the first telecommuter, linking up his bank and his home with the new phones.

» **1973**: Jack Nilles, rocket scientist, coins the terms "telecommute" and "telework." Nilles estimates that at this point there are "maybe a couple of thousand telecommuters" in the US.

» **1978**: Blue Cross/Blue Shield of South Carolina starts its "cottage-keyer" project for insurance claims data clerks. Results suggest productivity rises by over 25% compared to office-based workers.

» **1980**: Jack Nilles estimates there are 100,000 telecommuters in the US.

» **1981**: The IBM PC is launched – the machine that initiated the personal computer revolution, putting affordable computing on desks, and soon in homes, everywhere.

» **Mid-1980s**: Portable computers, if still the size of sewing machines, begin to make headway as a practical means of taking the office with you.

» **1986**: JALA (Nilles' consultancy, the name being derived from his and his partner's forenames, *Jack* and *Laila*) estimates US telecommuter population at 517,000.

» **1987**: US telecommuter population reaches 690,000, according to JALA.

» **1990**: New York research consultancy FIND/SVP estimates the number of telecommuters in the US has reached 3.4 million.

» **1991**: Alvin Toffler, author of *Future Shock*, publishes *The Third Wave*, envisaging a future of homeworking in electronic cottages equipped with computers and telecoms equipment.

» **1992**: EU Telework Forum sponsors the first European telework conference in the Netherlands.

» **1994**: FIND/SVP estimates that there are 9.1 million telecommuters in the US.

» **1997**: Estimated number of telecommuters in the US rises to 13 million (FIND/SVP). An AT&T/ITAC research study concludes that AT&T saves $3000 (about £1900) per teleworker annually in real estate and associated costs.

» **1999**: EU survey shows that Finland already has over 10% of its workforce teleworking.

» **2000**: ITAC announces that with the remote workforce swelling by 2.8 million over the previous year it had now reached the figure of 23.6 million teleworkers nationwide.

» **2004**: US and EU predicted to reach 30 million telecommuters each (ITAC).

» **2007**: EU predicted to reach 40 million telecommuters (ITAC).

» **2010**: US predicted to reach 40 million telecommuters (ITAC).

KEY LEARNING POINTS

» While the arrival of the personal computer is often seen as the start of remote working, the story actually goes back at least a century before.

» That said, the home computer, and the penetration of the Internet into industrial society, have proved to be the biggest facilitating technologies for remote working.

» Although still seen as something of an oddity, the growth of US teleworking suggests that some 40 million Americans will work remotely to some extent within a few years.

» Meanwhile Europe, although initially behind the US, looks set to overtake it in remote working in the very near future.

» Teleworking is not, however, for everyone or for every business culture, as the example of Japan shows.

The E-Dimension

This chapter highlights the extraordinary growth of the Internet and its implications both for companies and for the individual workers involved in remote work.

GROWTH OF THE INTERNET

It should be clear from Chapter 3 that the evolution of teleworking preceded that of the Internet by nearly a century, and the number of teleworkers in the US had exceeded 3.4 million before the Web became the commercial entity it is today. Nonetheless, there can be no doubting the effect that electronic communications have had on remote working, and it seems reasonable to suppose that the huge jump in American teleworkers from 3.4 million in 1990 to 9.1 million in 1994 is related to the rapid take-up of the Internet during that same period.

For remote working, the adoption of the Internet provides a highly efficient means of connecting workers and workplace; one that is available not only in every major city in the world, but also directly into a significant number of private households. Ten years ago the idea of a remote dial-up connection to a central computer was something understood only by technicians, and regularly done only by a select technocracy, what Nicholas Negroponte (founder of MIT Media Labs) referred to as the *digirati*. Now it is something that is taken for granted by the 400 million-plus Internet users around the world. CyberAtlas (www.cyberatlas.com) reports that the first quarter 2001 *Global Internet Trends* report from *Nielsen Net Ratings* measured Internet use in 27 countries around the world and found that 420 million people have Internet access.

These findings showed that the US and Canada still account for the largest proportion of the world's Internet access, with 41% of the global audience located in these countries. Europe, the Middle East, and Africa are responsible for 27% of the world's Internet population, followed by Asia Pacific (20%) and Latin America (4%).

"In terms of penetration levels, just over one-quarter of European households have Internet access via a home PC, compared to one-third of the households in Asia Pacific and nearly half of American households," said Richard Goosey, chief of measurement science and analytics at ACNielsen eRatings.com.

Of those who reported having Internet access, the number who had access from home was significant and often around, or over, the 50% mark. In both the UK and Ireland it was 46%, in Finland 49%,

Australia 50%, New Zealand 51%, Norway 53%, the Netherlands 56%, South Korea 57%, Denmark 58%, and Sweden 61%.

The fact that so many homes in these countries have Net access is of enormous importance to the future of remote working.

IMPLICATIONS FOR THE EMPLOYER

Not all jobs are suitable for teleworking, let alone full-time teleworking, but for most knowledge-based work there is a sizeable portion which lends itself to off-site work. The standardization of tools means that most knowledge-based workers use a portable computer, be it Mac or PC, and standard applications such as word processors, spreadsheets, CAD/CAM packages, etc. In some cases collaborative workers may need full-time access to a network of other workers' projects. In many, however, knowledge-based work requires occasional access to a central information source, the ability to work on it locally as an individual, and then occasional access again to send back the results of the individual work. The explosive growth of the Internet into the homes of the developed world means that almost all of the tools needed to satisfy that work pattern are already in place. Even more remarkable from the point of view of the employer is that, unlike the computer systems installed in workplaces, the ones set up at home are largely paid for by the individual worker.

ITAC reports that 46% of the teleworkers pay for both their equipment and its maintenance, with the employer covering all costs in only 29% of the cases (the costs being shared in the remaining 25% of cases). Other research studies suggest that the number of teleworkers buying their own equipment may be over 50%. This is no small figure, given that teleworkers tend to be heavier-than-average users of technology compared to other workers. In the US, ITAC reports that:

> "The average ownership pattern for home-only teleworkers is one PC for work, another for non-work purposes, 2.6 TVs, and 1.9 VCRs, as contrasted to an average of 0.8 PCs for work, 0.5 for non-work, and about the same number of TVs and VCRs for non-teleworkers. Yet, the top three non-computer technologies in use by teleworkers, in decreasing order of popularity, are the telephone, pager, and fax. Half the teleworkers use e-mail at least

three hours per week, but the average is seven hours because of some heavy users."

Nor is it just the initial cost of the technology that is being shouldered by the individual. According to ITAC, less than 20% of the teleworkers get intensive training in the use of their technology. The facts that home and work machines tend to be largely identical, that the applications on them are the same, and that there is familiarity with Internet access, mean that teleworking often involves little or no output on the part of the company in terms of materials or training. As AT&T notes:

"Interestingly, on the subject of knowledge transfer, we've seen decreasing demand for teleworker training. In fact, our classroom training for teleworkers and managers has been discontinued for lack of demand. Although an important part of our program ten years ago, before the rise of the knowledge economy, in this age of the PC and the Internet people seem to be more confident in their ability to work from home. Once telework is established as part of the culture, the formal processes such as training are less critical."
Dr. Braden Allenby AT&T's VP Environment, Health and Safety
Testimony to Congress March 22, 2001

Teleworkers seem to be as prepared to pay for their own ICT as conventional commuters are to pay for the car that they use to go to work.

On the other side of the equation, the benefits of a teleworker using a personal machine and Internet access are enormous. There are considerable productivity gains associated with teleworking, largely due to the fact that teleworkers are less likely to be interrupted, or feature in absenteeism reports. ITAC calculates that:

"The self-reported productivity improvement of home-based tele-workers averages 15% (the figure is 30% for telework-center-based teleworkers). This translates to an average annual bottom line impact of $9712 per teleworker. With 16.5 million teleworkers in the US that works out to an annual national impact exceeding $160 bn."

Other figures corroborate this. According to consultant Charles Grantham (president of the non-profit Institute for the Study of Distributed Work in Oakland, CA), companies save $2 for every $1 invested in remote equipment and extra phone lines. Elsewhere, typical figures include an average reduction in overhead per employee of $12,000 (T. Kane, Kinetic Workplace Consulting Group, White Paper, *Does Your Organization Really Encourage Telecommuting?*, 1997). Jack Nilles calculates that "an employee working at home one or two days per week can save a corporation $6000–$12,000 per year."

Perhaps the most comprehensive single study of cost saving comes from AT&T, which embarked on its own project involving 30,000 employees. The AT&T project was more expensive than most since it did install computer and phone systems (the latter at cost, of course) as well as paying phone and fax bills. Installation costs were found to average around $4000 per employee, a figure depreciated over five years and added to the phone and fax bills to arrive at an annual cost for the project of $3,205,507. Which gave an overall calculation per annum of:

Real estate savings $6,333,124
Productivity gains (hours) $5,112,841
Productivity gains (efficiency) $3,127,617
Total $14,573,582
Less costs ($3,205,507)
Net annual gain $11,368,075

The Internet not only provides a means of communication from the teleworker to the company; it can also be the means of technical support and collaboration. Whiteboarding, in which more than one worker has access to a shared document, makes it possible for co-workers to collaborate, highlighting queries or making changes. Access to corporate intranets via dial-up enables workers to check central FAQ lists to resolve common problems. Remote control software means that if troubleshooting has to be done by technical support staff, they can take control of the user's machine, and find the source of problems without having to be *in situ*. Helpdesk staff and technical support can therefore also be remote workers. Even management can be decentralized and spun out. ITAC's findings suggest that three of every five teleworkers have local supervisors, while nearly one in five are supervised by someone out of State.

If the public nature of the Net helps with accessibility, it does pose a problem to the company in terms of security. If a remote worker with dial-up access to the Net can then access the company's internal systems, there is always a danger that an unauthorized user may try and do the same. There is also the problem that remote workers are not themselves working within the walled garden of security. Teleworkers at home or on the road are not protected by the company firewall, and are themselves responsible for the viral protection of the machine. If the machine also serves as a family machine it runs correspondingly higher risks of being contaminated with viruses or unsuitable material through browsing and game playing. It is worth remembering that a remote computer, even if intended purely as a work machine, often becomes a family one either by the slow creep of family pressure, or by kids taking it upon themselves to turn it into a games terminal.

In all of these cases the response has to be a mixture of technology and good practice. Most company computers will be protected by a firewall and virus shield software but it is equally important to run that protection out to remote machines, even if they are laptops on the road. Installing virus shields on all remote machines is a sensible company step, as is automatically upgrading them as often as their desk-bound peers. Where there is a gateway from the Web to the corporate intranet it must be password protected at the very least, and other systems of identification used where suitable. These can vary from smartcards to biometric systems of voice or even fingerprint identification (which it is now possible to add to a keyboard). If passwords alone are used then remote workers should be made aware of the risks of writing them down, or using the same password for public Websites and having the computer store those passwords on the hard drive.

IMPLICATIONS FOR THE INDIVIDUAL WORKER

The implications of remote working by Web for the individual go beyond daytime TV, unlimited access to the fridge, or "that'll be me, by the pool." The first implication the Web brings, courtesy of its ubiquity, is the realization that, as Nilles puts it:

". . . every other American worker is a potential telecommuter."

"The US workforce can be grouped into four main categories: agriculture, industry/manufacturing, service, and information. The Census Bureau and the Bureau of Labor Statistics only use the first three, lumping information in with service. If we define the information sector as comprising those who make substantial portions of their income by creating, manipulating, transforming, and/or transmitting information, or operating information machines (such as computers) then about 60% of the US workforce fits that category in 1996. And the fraction is slowly growing."

"The main candidates for telecommuting are information workers. After all, as information technology (telecommunications and computers) becomes better and more pervasive, ever more jobs depend on it. However, some information jobs currently are not suited to any form of telecommuting. These include actors, some salespeople, and some teachers, for example. But I estimate that about 80% of the information workforce could telecommute at least some of the time. That works out to about 48% of the total workforce, or about every other American worker."

Not only are large numbers of workers potential teleworkers, but a large number of them are keen to join their ranks. In April 2001 a survey in the UK conducted by MORI (see Chapter 9) showed that nearly 30% of UK employees want to telework, and that 30% would consider changing jobs, and 25% would take a salary cut in order to be allowed to telework. The main reasons given were that it would exclude the worst of work – named as commuting time by 41% of respondents, office politics by 37%, and "constant interruptions" by 33%.

Graham Bevington, managing director of Mitel Networks, the company that sponsored the survey, concluded that: "The discovery that workers are increasingly dissatisfied with the office culture is not surprising. The increase in mobile and messaging technology means that employees have the tools necessary to be able to work from wherever they are. This coupled with the recent travel crises in the UK add to the frustration of having to come into the office day after day."

For many potential teleworkers the Web is the enabling tool that lets them dream of avoiding all the above-cited irritations of work. What they don't always immediately realize is that working remotely by Web does bring its own complications.

The first is that "working from home" can not only rid the worker of office politics and "the Company," but of company altogether. Solitary work often leaves individuals feeling out of the loop, and unable to get a perspective on problems by sharing "war stories" with fellow workers. Out of sight and out of mind is not a pleasant feeling when major changes are taking place in a company. Worse, company culture may mean that remote workers are not as highly valued as those who can be seen on the other side of the office. "Working from home" to some ranks with "food poisoning" as an invented excuse for not turning up to work.

Bizarrely, the opposite problem can also occur – too much company. Friends and family are often guilty of not taking homework seriously, or believing that, because a worker is at home, they are also at home to visitors. It takes a fair amount of discipline, applied both to self and to others, in order to ensure the potential productivity gains of remote work.

The answer to much of this lies in communications, in letting others know what you are doing and what you are contributing. Face-to-face meetings become more, not less, important if the virtual worker wants to avoid being peripheralized. Another solution may be to work in a satellite office or an *ad hoc* office used by other remote workers, whether for the same company or not. Having a workspace separate from the home can be a lifesaver. For tips on managing the work/life balance as a teleworker see the resources section (Chapter 9).

BEST PRACTICE

British Telecom (BT) launched its largest teleworking initiative, Options 2000, on July 1, 1999, with the aim of doubling the number of teleworkers each year. Originally the drive for this initiative came from the goal of reducing operating costs, but as the project matured it became clear that, as important as costs were, there was an equally significant improvement to be gained in productivity through worker satisfaction.

Certainly the initial response was markedly enthusiastic, with 3500 people registering to become teleworkers in the first 60 days. The company has replied by providing laptops to enable work from home, on the move, and from clients' premises. Integrated fax, scanner and printer units, and mobile phones were also provided, and the glue binding together all the communications technology was the company's intranet, claimed to be the largest in Europe. One feature of the intranet at BT is the "virtual number solution," which seamlessly locates staff by their phone number so that co-workers can find and collaborate with more mobile peers. The intranet was also used to Webcast business TV as part of the drive to keep all staff up to speed on developments and company thinking, regardless of location.

According to BT results have been impressive: "it is estimated that work productivity has been increased by 20% (data based on the previous initiatives). Furthermore, there was a positive impact on the environment, quality of work life, and employees' morale."

Enthusiasm for the scheme showed no sign of fading and within a year BT had notched up approximately 4000 teleworkers and 40,000 remote-access users.

The key points that seem to have ensured the success of the scheme are a combination of planning, preparation, and follow-up. Planning was the task of a joint program team which included specialists not just from ICT but also from facilities management and human resources. The full support of the board was secured to ensure that there was top-down understanding of goals and practices. Then work began on ensuring bottom-up understanding and support. The scheme was preceded by a comprehensive promotional campaign raising awareness about telework and its benefits. Once under way, the use of regular questionnaires and focus group interviews measured productivity and kept tabs on the project's development.

KEY LEARNING POINTS

» The cost and technology hurdles to remote working have been brought crashing down by widespread Internet access.

» That in turn makes teleworking ever more appealing to companies who can realize even greater savings in real estate, infrastructure, and absenteeism.

» Productivity increases more than outweigh initial investment.

» For the individual the perceived benefit is so great that many are happy to pay for their own home computers.

» Close consultation before and throughout the process is key to successful telework projects.

The Global Dimension

Starting with the issues of global remote working for companies, this chapter takes a look at the development and possibilities of virtual call-centers, the ability for single companies to span entire continents, and the feasibility of turning traditional challenges, such as different time zones, into a competitive advantage. The second part of the chapter looks at what globalization means for individuals, particularly in terms of matching skill-sets to jobs (wherever they may be), and the role of the mobile worker: the road warrior.

GLOBAL REMOTE WORKING FOR COMPANIES

Globalization and remote working were made for each other on a number of levels. As companies expand into other national markets they necessarily expand their organizations to the point where physical presence and face-to-face meetings are no longer the most important link between central managers and local workers. At the same time, the very nature of the World Wide Web offers a platform for communication across continents but still for the cost of a local call. Satellite offices in other parts of the world may become a necessity, and in the process remote collaboration becomes part and parcel of company culture.

In addition, the task of serving global markets often brings in two other factors of globalization: language and time differences. Having clients in different time zones may require local offices to serve them, but even with that in place it is not always possible to duplicate the full range of services provided by the central office. A Californian company, with a full service call-center, is going to be of little use answering customer queries in the UK, and even a local sales office in London may not answer the need.

Add language barriers to that mix and it becomes ever more complex. The need for multilingual customer support has already driven the development of the call-center industry, and provided high employment in areas such as Ireland where good local language skills combine with relatively cheap real estate. Now we are increasingly seeing a new industry springing up in the form of the virtual call-center – also called a Personal Branch Exchange (PBX) extender. Instead of having to find an affordable location, then attract suitably talented people to it, the technology allows incoming calls and their associated client details to be distributed electronically to computer-equipped operators who can be in any geographical location. Agents in a decentralized virtual call-center can be spread across different time zones to offer a 24/7 service. They can speak different languages and have calls routed to them on the basis of that, and, since all the agents use a Web browser as a terminal, a remote agent is indistinguishable from an in-office one as far as the customer is concerned.

The most dramatic examples of this are provided by such companies as 247customer.com and CustomerAsset.com, both in India. They train up English-speaking staff to deal with calls from the US, including acquiring the right form of answering (done by studying *Friends* and *Seinfeld*, apparently). When a US caller dials the 1–800 number or picks up the phone to find themselves talking to an American-sounding woman selling goods and services, they are not aware that they are actually speaking to an operator based just outside Bangalore.

Remote working enables an organization to harness ability wherever it may be, instead of being forced to recruit locally. Global markets make that reach truly global and the Net allows it to happen. Take the case of Wipro in Bangalore, India. Wipro started out manufacturing cooking fat but moved into software nearly 20 years ago and now specializes in providing long-distance programming. *Wired Magazine* (8.03–March 2000 issue) reports that:

"Most of Wipro's action takes place in 30 football-field-sized offices in Bangalore, Chennai, and Hyderabad – what the company has dubbed 'offshore development centers.' They operate on a simple idea: thanks to the Net, it's possible to turn an office in India into an extension of a client's own development and maintenance center for software. Premji [the company CEO] invented the idea of servicing the world's computers from India, where the cost of labor is one-tenth of that in the States. And because Bangalore is ten-and-a-half hours ahead of New York, Wipro programmers can work on US computers at night so they're ready the next morning."

When the Y2K bug was occupying the minds of IT departments the world over, the talent pool in India was kept busy working for companies on the other side of the world. Or to be more specific, the other end of the time zone range, because one of the key points of this remote work is that it can be used in partnership with local workers. On a big project like Y2K this enabled work to continue round the clock without anyone doing a night shift – one team on one side of the globe would clock off at the end of the day and hand over the work done to another international team as they clocked on.

Similarly the narrow streets of Soho, London, are full of sound and video editing houses, specializing in animated special effects, and digital sound mixing. As well as having the talent pool they also have time on their side, at least as far as Hollywood is concerned. The time difference means that a scene has been shot it can be pumped down the transatlantic pipeline and into a high-speed local network called SohoNet, set up by and for the editing houses. There they can parcel out the work and create effects or finish edits which, with a five-hour time difference, they can hand back in the afternoon local time, and still be in time for the start of the working day back on the West Coast of the US. June Langhoff (in *The Telecommuter's Advisor*, Aegis, 1996) gives the example of another Hollywood project conducted remotely: "Actor Nick Nolte worked on a sound-dubbing project with his director, Charles Shyer, for the 1994 movie, *I Love Trouble*. Though the final mix sounded like they were in the same studio, they were actually 6000 miles apart, with Shyer in Burbank, Nolte in Paris."

Nor is globalization only an issue for large corporations looking for alternative labor forces. The ability to work remotely also has major effects on individuals.

GLOBAL REMOTE WORKING FOR INDIVIDUALS

In the global context there are two main types of individual remote workers: those who choose to work for a company that is in a remote location to them, and those who, whether they normally work remotely for a company or not, now find themselves needing to stay in touch while on the move.

Of the former, Jack Nilles notes that "as the costs of transport (read telecommunications) become small relative to the cost of labor, then there is a great incentive/temptation to look beyond one's own back yard for the necessary expertise."

Which is precisely what the Dallas Museum of Art did according to June Langhoff: "The Dallas Museum of Art searched far and wide for the best expert on European art when it hired Dorothy Kosinski as curator, even though she continues to live in Basel, Switzerland. Long-distance relationships also avoid the costs of relocation, estimated at around $80,000 per employee."

Similarly, the ability to telework can mean the ability to hang on to highly skilled personnel even though their personal situation takes them away from the office, or even the country. For some years Nick Shelness was chief technology officer of Lotus Development Corp.

Although a familiar face at important Lotus meetings and development conferences as far afield as Lotusphere Florida and Lotusphere Berlin, he was nonetheless based in a remote mill in Scotland.

For most of us, however, the impact of globalization on remote working is ironically just the opposite – that we have to travel physically, and yet still remain in touch with the office. The travelling remote worker, or "road warrior," is much in evidence at airports and on trains, usually identified by the distinctive tapping of laptop keys or the urgent pressing of mobile phone buttons in the attempt to get a signal.

Globalization has had a few effects on their remote working patterns too. While there remain problems associated with the different types of networks used for mobile phones worldwide, dual-band phones (allowing European and African roaming) and triple-band phones (which allow the above plus the US) mean that there are a sufficient number of customers for the mobile phone companies to set up roaming agreements. Roaming agreements between the home operator and those in foreign countries allow users to continue using their mobile as they go, simply logging on to foreign networks which bill back to the original operator. The use of mobile computers, already well-established with the laptop format, has been boosted by the arrival of lightweight devices based around cut-down operating systems. Windows CE, the slimmed down version of Windows, allows devices such as the Compaq Aero which looks like a laptop but has no moving parts and weighs no more than a decent novel. Better yet, the growth in popularity of PDAs (Personal Digital Assistants) such as the Palm Pilot, combined with the roaming agreements for mobile phones, means that it is increasingly possible to go abroad, hook up the PDA to the mobile phone (either by wire or by infrared) and download e-mails. PDAs from companies including Palm and Psion also now have groupware clients such as Lotus Notes (see Chapter 8) available for them so that it is possible to call up on the mobile and not only receive e-mail but also perform groupware tasks including downloading details of meetings and synching with the office scheduler. The bandwidth restrictions of first generation (GSM) mobile phones are rapidly being overcome by the advent of accelerated GSM and eventually Third Generation (3G) mobiles across the globe – for more details see Chapter 6, The State of the Art.

While such technologies make totally mobile connectivity a possibility for remote working, it remains expensive and slow and will do for some time to come. The spread of the Web, however, means that it is also possible for the road warrior to link up via a local call, either by using a local ISP, or by signing up with one of the global providers (such as AOL) which guarantee access across large swathes of the planet. That still leaves the problem of physically connecting. In countries like the US, where road warriors are common, hotels usually provide a data jack in the wall or in the phone itself. In much of the rest of the world, however, and in almost all private accommodation, the globetrotting teleworker will have to plug in via a local phone socket. For advice on how to achieve that, regardless of the country or type of phone, see the road warrior resources section in Chapter 9.

One of the other boons of globalization for the remote worker is that the mushrooming of cybercafés means that it may not be necessary to struggle with portable equipment and alien phone jacks at all. Cybercafés provide a simple and cheap means of getting online and sending or downloading data. In many cities there are cybercafés specifically targeting the remote worker, with quiet environments, dedicated graphics workstations for those who need them, scanners, and of course printers or CD writers. Such cybercafés function much like a commercial telecenter and have preferential tariffs for those who intend to stay online for a long time. In order to ensure that there is a functioning cybercafé that will fulfill your needs, it's strongly recommended to use a cybercafé search engine to find one (see search engines in Chapter 9 – Resources) and then to get in touch with it before you go to ensure it's currently in operation. Bear in mind as well that Web access is only part of the story and if you will need to access a remote intranet, or retrieve corporate e-mail, then these systems will have to be set up with a password-protected gateway before you go. It pays to have fallbacks, such as setting up a Web-based mail account so that in the event that you can't use your company's internal system you at least have a means of sending and receiving mail and files as you move. Depending on the work that is being done, it may also be worthwhile to set up a virtual office and meeting space. These are available via commercial sites which provide the facilities for online conferencing, chat, task assignment, goal scheduling, and document management, all accessible by browser. For a list of online office tools see remote worker resources in Chapter 9.

BEST PRACTICE

There are many different reasons for international teleworking, but access to talented individuals in remote locations is one of the most satisfying. The case of Lotus fellow Nick Shelness is a good example in that it brings out management as well as technical issues involved in teleworking across time zones.

"Fellow" is the highest rank of technologist at both IBM and Lotus and Shelness was a fellow at both. He was also for some time the chief technical officer of Lotus Development, a company based in Boston, Massachusetts, but, as Shelness explained to *Fast Company* magazine, changes in his private life meant that he no longer felt he could work in the US.

"My wife and I live in a renovated late seventeenth-century corn mill 60 miles *[about 95 km]* north of Edinburgh, Scotland - and about 3500 miles *[about 5600 km]* from Lotus headquarters. We moved there in 1991 - four years after my wife had surgery for a neurological condition. During most of those four years, she spent about a third of her time in the hospital. Even so, before we moved, she was still running the molecular medicine lab at the College of Physicians and Surgeons at Columbia University. Her neurologist told her, 'We can't guarantee that if you stop working, you'll get better. But if you don't stop, we can guarantee that you won't.' She's Scottish, so we moved to Scotland."

Lotus is an unusual case in that its main product is groupware – software that enables people to collaborate even at a distance – so it would have been something of an admission of failure to lose a member of staff to geography. Instead it was decided that Shelness would work remotely, with Lotus Notes as his main messaging and scheduling tool. Lotus also creates remote collaboration spaces – virtual meeting rooms if you like – and knowledge management tools that help workers find who the experts are in a field, wherever they may be located geographically, and put them in touch. Having established the technology bridge, the next factor consisted of dealing with the time zone. This was turned to advantage by working around a quiet period in Shelness' morning when the US had yet to log on, then spending the afternoon communicating.

> "I spend about a third of each year on the road. The rest of the time, I work from my home, where I have four computers. In the morning, I can work uninterrupted, but in the afternoon, I'm constantly communicating. To keep my travel load to a minimum while making sure that the CEO knows my activities, I submit weekly reports detailing what I've accomplished."

Those reports highlight the other issue which is always present in remote working – that of communication and the importance of staying in the loop – though Shelness added that it was also a feature of his own self-discipline.

> "In truth, those reports are more for me than for him. Having a written record of what I've done is very valuable. When you work at home, it's easy to feel ineffectual. If you're at home reading and thinking, and the phone isn't ringing, it's easy to lose track of what you've accomplished. Maybe people with huge egos don't have that problem, but I do."

In technology terms Lotus had it easy, though all of the tools used are commercially available. From the point of view of best practice, what matters here is not the tools, but the careful use of time zones to best advantage, the structured emphasis on communication, and the discipline that the worker imposed on himself – all points that remain true for any remote worker.

KEY LEARNING POINTS

» For organizations the global factor means that truly remote sites can be set up to make use of language and time barriers - work can become truly 24-hour.

» It is possible to cherry-pick skills wherever they may be found instead of recruiting from a purely local skill pool.

» Remote working can be the key to retaining skilled workers.

» Teleworking means a key team member is still part of the team on the road, or on another continent.

The State of the Art

A chapter which looks at the technologies reshaping the way we work and in particular the local radio network technology Bluetooth, the potential of third generation telephony bringing broadband to the mobile handset, and of DSL and satellite bringing broadband to the home. The future of virtual conferencing, tele-immersion, is considered, as well as the importance of both Virtual Private Networks and Voice-over IP for the future of virtual and decentralized companies.

BLUETOOTH

Named after the Viking king who united Denmark in the late 900s, Bluetooth looks to become the wireless standard that not only does away with the "spaghetti" of local networks but makes sense of the swelling ranks of portable devices that load down today's road warrior. As well as converting them to Christianity, Harald Bluetooth managed to distract the horn-helmeted folks from the traditional joys of pillaging and get them to talk to each other. For which he is immortalized as a short-range radio frequency specification developed jointly by such companies as Ericsson, IBM, Toshiba, Nokia, and Motorola. One Bluetooth-equipped device will automatically recognize another that is within range and the two can then talk to each other and see if they can work together. In practice that has a number of possible benefits for road warriors and remote workers.

A Bluetooth-enabled mobile phone would be able to recognize that you had just walked into your own home. It would then link up with the Bluetooth-enabled phone in your home and re-route the call you're making via the (much cheaper) land line. A Bluetooth-enabled PDA or portable would be able to look around you for other devices that could help you do work. Which means that if you walked into an office and hit the print button on your portable it would use radio to find the nearest printer and print without anything having to be plugged in or configured. Right now, if you have an ordinary PDA without a modem attached you can write e-mails but you can't send them. If the same PDA was Bluetooth-enabled you could hit "send" and it would effectively go through your pockets and search the nearby area until it found that Bluetooth mobile phone in your jacket on the back of the chair. The two would then be able to work together to send your data. What the makers envisage is a Personal Area Network (PAN) of radio signals around you so that all the different devices that a road warrior currently carries can make the most of each other. That way your PDA can access the phone even though it is in your briefcase, while the wireless headphones playing music from a MiniDisc in your pocket will switch to the phone if a call happens to come in.

Science fiction? Not for much longer it seems. Bluetooth was first demonstrated in 1998 and, while it has been slow to make it to market, the first generation of products is appearing now. Bluetooth headsets mean that mobile phone users can keep their phone in their pocket and still speak using wire-free microphones. Bluetooth networks are being created so that they can transmit information and relay e-mails whenever a worker with a Bluetooth device comes within range, meaning that you can receive messages even with your phone switched off and your PDA stowed somewhere at the bottom of a bag. In London there is a network company busy Bluetooth-enabling a station and its trains. In Dallas there is a bar with Bluetooth networking in it so that remote workers can load up on e-mails simply by sitting down and having a beer. Bluetooth home networks mean that all your mobile devices can access the printer or scanner without you having to wire them up or configure them. For remote workers dropping into telecenters or satellite offices, that would be a huge boon as well as a relatively cheap and efficient means of sharing peripherals.

There are problems, however. The radio frequency chosen is cheap and easy to implement but won't work in France where it is currently reserved for military use and in the US there is a risk of interference thanks to the frequency also being used by the remote controls for garage doors. Nonetheless, the names behind the project, and the tumbling cost of technology, mean that Bluetooth is likely to go from gadget freak must-have to high-street reality within the next couple of years.

THIRD GENERATION TELEPHONY – BROADBAND TO THE HANDSET

Even for an industry that delights in arcane acronyms the next step in mobile telephony is almost wilfully obscure in its names and terms. Without getting too bogged down by the terms being bandied around (UMTS, GPRS, Gen2.5, 3G, etc.), what really matters about the next step is bandwidth and data.

The arrival of 3G is awaited with much excitement, not so much because it will simply be faster and better than current mobile telephony, but because it will be sufficiently fast to bring together the two areas of mobile phone use and the Internet. Since these are the two technologies that have done the most in recent years to liberate the remote worker, the advent of 3G is potentially one of the most exciting developments in years for remote workers and road warriors alike.

The first generation of mobile phones was the analogue cell-phone. The second was the digital GSM phone, but even though the system is digital it was not designed with data traffic in mind and so data throughput on a GSM phone was limited to 9.6 kilobits per second. Compare that to a standard modem at 56.6 kilobits per second and you can see that whilst it can cope with sending e-mails it just isn't up to the job of surfing the Net or sending and receiving large files. Enter GPRS (General Packet Radio Service) which takes existing GSM services and allows for 56.6 kilobits per second data transfer rates and an always-on connection. In the UK GPRS, and its rival HSCSD (High Speed Circuit Switched Data), are both on offer, but are only seen as a half-way house, just pumped-up GSM (hence their occasionally being referred to as Gen2.5), while the market still waits for true 3G (sometimes also called UMTS in Europe – Universal Mobile Telecommunications System).

As well as the promise of megabit connectivity, 3G is expected to enable multimedia applications including video-telephony and broadcast (the rights to broadcast football games over 3G have already been sold in the UK). 3G will be able to charge on the basis of data sent and received, rather than minutes on a call and so will be a permanently-on solution and will be able to channel data and calls so that the same handset can have more than one number and more than one billing account – enabling personal use and a business account, for example. 3G should also be able to offer far more accurate pinpointing of the user, which in turn allows for location-based services, such as the ability to ask your 3G phone, PDA, or laptop where the nearest cash machine or service station is. Most crucially for the remote worker, it is likely to usher in a new generation of always-on, broadband mobile Internet terminals in ever smaller formats. This could make videoconferencing a possibility even for the road warrior, which would go a long way towards helping remote collaboration.

Most important of all, by providing a standard national platform for broadband wireless, it is thought that 3G may prove the catalyst that moves business away from wires in such applications as Local Area Networks (LANs). Currently, in order for workers to connect to the internal network, they have to plug into a jack, with all the infrastructure costs that that implies and the limited workstations that it imposes. If LANs were to run over 3G wireless then the LAN jack would become redundant, and with that it would mean that a remote worker returning to the office would no longer have to look for a place to dock before they could work. Better yet, it makes for a cheap and flexible way of providing the necessary LAN infrastructure for telework centers, allowing companies to experiment, or set up and disband telework centers wherever they choose and at relatively little expense. That in turn is likely to have a major impact on the way teams are formed and work.

It's not all smooth sailing though. At £22.5bn (about $36trn) the cost of the five British 3G licenses has pushed telecoms companies into debt. In addition the likelihood that the US and Europe will opt for different systems means that global roaming will only be a reality if handsets are designed to work on both systems. All of which means that technology which should have been with us already is still expected to be restricted to a privileged few for the next couple of years.

DSL/SATELLITE – BROADBAND TO THE HOME

Digital Subscriber Line (DSL) technology, whether it be Asymmetric DSL (ADSL) or its stable-mate Symmetric DSL (SDSL), is widely touted as the answer to the problem of rolling out affordable broadband to the home. This is true wherever ordinary copper phone lines are used, but particularly so in Europe where cable hasn't had the success it has enjoyed in the US.

ADSL is the most commonly encountered flavor of DSL, and can offer a downstream rate (i.e. *to* the home or business) of anywhere from two to eight megabits per second, and an upstream (i.e. *from* the home or business) of up to 640 kilobits per second, although the more normal offering is only 256 kilobits per second. It's because of that difference in upstream and downstream that the technology is called asymmetric. This works simply because most of us download more data and media than we create, though in some cases, especially videoconferencing, it may be necessary to have greater throughput in both directions, in which case SDSL (symmetric) is used to provide a stream in both directions which is typically much lower than the usual ADSL downstream, but higher than its upstream. It should be remembered that even the slowest ADSL upstreams are generally some four times faster than the fastest dial-up modems, and double the speed of ISDN (Integrated Services Digital Network). Since DSL doesn't require a dedicated line it is much cheaper than its slower rival ISDN. As well as providing access in areas that haven't been cabled, it rivals cable modem speeds for access. Most important of all it goes beyond that and rivals expensive leased lines for throughput on downloads – which has given rise to a problem since phone companies have proved less than keen to roll out a technology which makes their more expensive solutions redundant at a stroke.

For the home worker, however, DSL looks to be the ideal solution since they already have phone lines in place and so don't need to wait while expensive dedicated lines are run out to their building. It is an always-on solution so there is no limitation to the time they spend online and it doesn't interfere with simultaneous phone calls in or out. The available bandwidth makes videoconferencing a reality, as well as permitting the sending and downloading of large files. Because the throughput speeds are sufficient for the streaming of full-speed full-motion video, ADSL has become increasingly common as a means of delivering video-on-demand services. As the number of DSL-equipped exchanges grows, so do the possibilities for high-speed home access. It can also be a major factor in the decision to embark on a policy of satellite offices or telecottaging since it means a very cheap way of equipping a new location with high bandwidth.

The main catch for the remote worker is that the permanently-on nature of the connection makes it even more important to have proper security protection in place if sensitive data is being transmitted. For further consideration of security see the following discussion of Virtual Private Networks (VPNs).

Satellite Internet access is another solution to the bandwidth bottle-neck, albeit one with even more pronounced asymmetry than ADSL. The idea of satellite Net access is much like satellite TV. The user needs a dish, and a decoder card in their computer, with the aid of which they can download data at megabits per second speeds. The joy of satellite is that it can provide a high bandwidth connection even for relatively remote areas or isolated individuals for whom the arrival of cable, or even a DSL-equipped phone exchange, remains a distant dream. The downside is that while the downstream to the user is counted in megabits, the upstream is provided by nothing more advanced than a standard dial-up connection over the phone line. Not only does this mean a restriction to 56 kilobits per second but it also ties up the phone line in service, making it necessary to have a second line installed if work involves having both online access and voice traffic at the same time.

TELE-IMMERSION – POTENTIAL USE OF BROADBAND

Tele-immersion is the step beyond simple teleconferencing. Rather than have a reduced image of your correspondent on a screen, the idea is that the scene in front of you is so realistic that you appear to be there, as part of a meeting that may be taking place on the other side of the world. The goal of tele-immersion is to allow those people to feel as if they are sharing the same physical space and in the process overcome some of the limitations of conventional videoconferencing.

Creating the impression of remote individuals, also called a "tele-presence," clearly requires a little more than a normal computer screen or a videophone. In the US the National Tele-Immersion Initiative (NTII), has already trialed a system which enabled a researcher in New York to feel as if he was looking across a deskful of people even though in reality those people were in Pennsylvania. Digital cameras and laser range-finders were used to capture the movements of the people gathered around the desk, then transmitted over a high-speed link to New York. The researcher sat in front of two screens and wore special glasses much like an updated version of the green and red lens glasses used in 3D cinemas. The glasses polarized the image so that one eye saw one picture, the other eye registered another image from a different perspective, and in his mind the researcher was able to form a 3D image. Movement sensors followed the way the researcher's head moved and updated the images being shown on screen accordingly. The result is said to be life-size 3D imaging, meaning that you can realistically move your head to one side to look around a person on screen and see who or what is behind them.

Due to the sheer amount of specialized equipment, the computing power, and the bandwidth requirements, this remains a laboratory project only, but the implication is clear that it may be possible to have immersive meetings in the future in which all the subtleties of body language are retained. Project teams could move around a piece of engineering and look at it as if it were on a table in front of them. People on a number of different locations could appear to be assembled at the same desk, with the object of discussion in front of them.

Across the Atlantic in Europe is a similar project called VIRTUE (VIRtual Team User Environment) which aims to develop the technology necessary to produce a convincing impression of presence in a semi-immersive teleconferencing system that uses large flat panel video walls to create the impression that you are sitting opposite your remote collaborators. To get a more vivid idea of what that would be like, take a look at the Shockwave animation of VIRTUE at www3.btwebworld.com/virtue/NewPublicArea/publicity.htm

VIRTUAL PRIVATE NETWORKS (VPN)

The idea behind VPNs is that private networks, such as the standard office LAN, are secure and reliable but are very expensive to run out to a remote location. Public networks, meaning the Internet, are already in place and thus cheap and easy as a way of networking remote individuals, but they have the problem that by their nature they pose major security risks. The idea of a VPN is to provide the access control and security of a private network while making use of the cheapness and availability of the Net.

A VPN, then, is a private connection made over a public network, which in daily life means that a worker in a satellite office in Dubai or a cybercafé in Cairo can dial up (at local call rates) and log on to the company's network as if they were in corporate headquarters. Behind the scenes that means that access control, authentication, encryption, and a technique called "tunneling" are needed to transfer company network data over alien networks that may be running on any combination of technologies. At no point should the public be able to see the private areas of the network, while those working in the private areas should not notice that their files are in fact charging off across the world to their colleagues.

There are two problems in all this – security and performance. Performance at best will be limited by the speed of the base network back at HQ. Chains are only as strong as their weakest link, however, and clearly if a remote worker is connecting via a GSM mobile phone then they will currently be limited to a data speed of 9.6 kilobits per second (at least until GSM is upgraded – see above). Which is not to say that remote workers are forced to endure treacle-slow access, just that it increases the desirability of high bandwidth access such as DSL or satellite (see above). Unfortunately, there is another factor in the performance, which is the security issue. Because of the need for encryption (scrambling the data in transfer), and the tunneling and addressing information (to ensure the data is routed to the right end-user), as much as a third of the data stream may consist of security and routing information, leaving only two-thirds of the bandwidth available for your actual data.

Nonetheless, the appeal of extending the company's firewall is obvious, effectively extending corporate defences out over the Internet and protecting sensitive data even as it flows around the world over the Net. Authentication technology is also getting better so that many systems employ a two-tier system whereby the user has to demonstrate both something they know (the classic password approach) and also something they have. The latter has traditionally been called a token and usually meant the likes of smart card. Increasingly, however, biometrics are coming into play so that keyboards are equipped with fingerprint scanners, or voice and face recognition are combined with Webcams to ensure that users are authenticated. Best of all, many ASPs (Application Service Providers) are stepping in to offer VPNs to companies that don't want to go through the process of developing their own.

Jack Nilles, the father of teleworking, argues that it boils down to complexity, security, and cost, concluding that:

"Complexity. If you either already have a real private network – and find that its costs and complexity are growing out of bounds – or you haven't the staff or budget to tackle what is essentially the task of running your own phone company, then a VPN may be an ideal solution."

"Security. If information security is the paramount considera-tion, with low-cost access to teleworkers, customers, and suppliers a close second, then VPNs are worth investigating. The market has a growing variety of security options, with various forms of encryption, authentication, and message encapsulation to protect your information."

"Cost. A primary attraction of the Internet and VPNs is the possibility of major telecomm costs savings. The level of savings is proportional to the amount of long distance telecommunications you need for your ordinary business and your teleworkers. If your company has leased telecomm lines (i.e., a private network) that are chronically operating below capacity except to peak periods, then you may find substantial savings by using a VPN either for all of your communications or for peak loads on top of a smaller private network. One problem of using VPNs with home-based teleworkers is that of access; some Internet Service Providers, such as Comcast's @Home service, refuse to allow VPN for home users connected via cable modems because of the bandwidth-hogging impacts. In those cases the alternative is to use DSL, if available, or settle for much slower dial-up connections."

Jack Nilles, Managing Telework, *chapter 4*

VOICE-OVER INTERNET PROTOCOL

Voice-over Internet Protocol (VoIP) started as Internet enthusiasts found that they could use a microphone and digitizing card in their computer to turn their voices into digital traffic which could be sent over the Internet and listened to at the other end by someone else even if they were based on the other side of the world. They in turn could speak into their microphone and reply, albeit with a delay that made the whole thing more reminiscent of CB radio calls than modern telephony. Why did they do this? Because Internet access involves only a local call, often free in the States, while long-distance calls continue to be expensive.

It wasn't long before companies with large long-distance bills twigged that there was a major cost saving to be had here, and the VoIP business began in earnest.

In order for voice traffic to travel over the Net it must first be turned into digital signals, but that is ever easier as sound-equipped computers can make the conversion in real time. It then has to be divided up into packets of data and sent over a network using Internet Protocol (hence the "IP"). That, too, is simple given that IP is the basic building block of most networks in use today. The catch is that it also requires the network technology to prioritize the voice traffic in order to avoid quality problems. If a normal file or e-mail takes some time to arrive it is not a major problem, but if the next sentence of a phone call is dawdling across the network then the sense of the communication is lost.

This in turn entails the cost of setting up a new communications technology at the heart of the company's server system, but in return the company can route phone calls to satellite offices and telecenters virtually for free. If those offices are on the other side of the globe, the VoIP technology can rapidly pay for itself and the usefulness in the field of remote working is obvious. Virtual call-centers in particular are proving quick to appreciate the benefits.

As well as cutting phone bills, the point of VoIP is that it is much easier to integrate with a computer system, and that can have benefits for such fields as security and mobility. For example, there is a daily newspaper in Scotland called *Business AM* which has satellite offices in Edinburgh, Glasgow, and London, all linked by a VoIP system. When a worker sits down at a desk, any desk in any location, they simply key in their password at that computer and the network knows to route all their calls to the phone by their side. That extension becomes their own, and so, combined with a VPN (see above), workers can move freely from one office to another as it suits them, and anyone collaborating with them or just calling up from outside will have no idea that they are not rooted to their desks at central office. So sophisticated is the system that it not only knows to route that person's calls to the phone nearest them, but also to instantly load it up with knowledge of all their rapid-dialing codes and saved phone numbers. It is possible to make a phone call in London one day, then go to Scotland another day and hit the redial button on the nearest phone which will then dial the same number dialed from London.

VoIP has had to struggle to overcome the issues of quality that plagued its early days, but the benefits to a virtual or distributed organization mean that it is certain to become ever more popular in the years to come.

For further information on the products and services available there is information at the sites of the major VoIP suppliers, including

Agilent (www.agilent.com), Cisco (www.cisco.com), and Nortel Bay (www.nortelnetworks.com).

KEY LEARNING POINTS

» While technology is not what defines remote working, new technologies are enabling new work practices and a more seamless integration of far-flung staff into a distributed organization.

» Broadband to the home and the handset mean that more complex media, including videoconferencing and tele-immersion, will continue to blur the boundaries between remote and local workers.

In Practice – Flexible and Virtual Working Success Stories

Taking a look at different approaches to remote working from around the globe, including remote working for remote areas – with examples from the Hebrides islands off Scotland – and the mathematics of savings for a large corporation, courtesy of AT&T. The best solutions for the individual road warriors are catered for with the NewsGear project while potential hurdles for remote working are observed at work in Japan.

REMOTE WORKING FOR REMOTE AREAS – LASAIR AND THE HEBRIDES

Some may choose remote working but for those in the Highlands and Islands of Scotland remoteness is something forced upon them. Teleworking has proved to be the answer for the workforce of the Western Isles, who came together in 1995 with the support of the European Union to count their blessings in the form of an audit of skills available in the region. It was found that they had an unusually high number of graduates and telecommunications infrastructure and so the potential for harnessing the knowledge skills by teleworking was clear. Emphasis was on two projects: a call-center at Stornoway, on the Isle of Lewis in the Outer Hebrides; and the creation of a virtual company called Lasair. The call-center originally created 70 jobs but work overload is directed to rural telework centers, which created another 25 jobs in the first year (1998). As well as call-center workers in the center, the creation of the venture also provided work for those with computer skills providing technical support.

The other venture, Lasair, is an even more remarkable example of remote working. Originally an editing and database compilation service, its flexibility has led to diversification into a number of areas. Among others, this has meant compiling database records for the Home Office Forensic Science Service based in London, and the editing of the *Grove Dictionary of Music*. That entails a team of 10 people on the island of Barra doing the mark-up work and then passing it on to the Lasair office on the island of Benbecula for quality control work. From there it is sent back to the publishers based in Oxford in the English Midlands.

Kathleen Turner, a director of Lasair, explains that:

"Being located where we are matters not at all. The telecommunications links are very well developed – the Highlands and Islands of Scotland are more advanced in some ways than some southern mainland UK regions – and we can undertake just anything these days. The Western Isles also has a higher percentage of graduates per capita than anywhere else in the country, so we've found it quite an advantage to be here."

"I think we've proved ourselves. For example, we have a contract with the Home Office Forensic Science Service to compile their database records. The work was previously done in London, and it took several weeks to turn the work around. We send it back in five days."

"We are in day-to-day communication with our contractors, mainly electronically. We run an e-mail conference, and as I receive information I put it out on to the conference: it could be updates of software, or files which need to be sent out. It means that people for whom it's relevant can pick it up immediately. We encourage people to check their e-mail regularly throughout the day."

The growth in online commerce has further added to Lasair's potential for remote working, as Turner explains in a UK Government study called *Working from Anywhere*:

"We are exploring new avenues of innovation to provide the ultimate virtual service solution. We have recently started a service, 'LiveGenie' to provide on-line interactive customer support services for busy web sites. 'LiveGenie' enables our clients to transform the manner in which buying, selling and customer support is conducted on their Internet sites."

The next step in Lasair's Web services project swiftly followed as the virtual company teamed up with Iomart, an ISP, to provide remote Web page creation and support services. The system works by Iomart contracting out Web consultants working as part of Iomart's Net Centre while being physically located in their homes in the Western Isles.

What makes it a great example of remote working at its best is the use of technology to make the most of human resources in an area that might otherwise have been thought disadvantaged by its location. Instead, a flexible approach to available work has been combined with appropriate use of the available technology to overcome the difficulties of the location. In the process the scheme manages to ensure the continuation of a community that might otherwise have suffered from decline as its population was forced to move to mainland cities to find work.

Time-line

» **Early 1990s**: the potential of new technology recognized as holding the key to developing a remote region with a highly qualified labor force.

» **1991**: LEADER 1 program launched by the European Commission to develop rural regions by encouraging the emergence of innovative local initiatives.

» **1995**: following a year of action research on opportunities for teleworking, an action plan was developed for the deployment of rural telework centers in local villages.

» **1998**: local skills register of 600 people living on, or hoping to live on, the islands showed over 50 had a degree or doctorate in science, engineering, or computer science.

» **1998**: by now Lasair, a private desktop publishing corporation and mandated to manage teleworking contracts, had a stable of 35 home-based teleworkers. All the workers are linked through an electronic network that provides for the exchange of information, the rapid transmission of new guidelines and contracts and knowledge update.

» **1998**: call-center established in Stornoway Business Park. Seventy jobs created and sales figures of $1.5 mn posted in its first year. The work overload is directed to rural telework centers, an extension of the call-center, which provided 25 jobs.

» **2000**: Lasair now employing 100 people scattered around the islands. Announces joint project with ISP Iomart to provide Web creation services remotely.

KEY LEARNING POINT

» What got this project off on the right foot was a process of careful consideration from the start. The initial study – an audit of work skills available in the area – made it clear that teleworking was an appropriate solution. By launching the call-center, the technical support service needed to maintain it, and the virtual company, the region made the most of a broad range of knowledge skills. A flexible mix of telecenter, home-working, and remote collaboration then ensured that the benefits of the work could be run out to inhabitants no matter where they lived in the cluster of islands.

ADDING UP THE NUMBERS – AT&T

As one of the world's most important telecoms providers, AT&T clearly has a vested interest in promoting telework, but it also faced the implicit challenge that if a telecoms company couldn't successfully use teleworking then how could it convince its clients. The gauntlet was thrown down for the company to put its methodology where its mouth was, becoming one of the pioneers of corporate teleworking in the process, and producing detailed accounts of how much money a corporation could save by the practice.

In March 2001 Dr Braden Allenby, AT&T's VP Environment, Health, and Safety, spelt out the history and results in a testimony to the US Congress as follows:

"AT&T started a pilot program in Los Angeles in 1989 and then in Phoenix in 1990 with a handful of employees trialing the idea of working from home several days per month, in part as a voluntary response to Title I of the 1990 Clean Air Act. We were motivated by the results of our pilot to expand the offer to more areas of the company. In 1992, AT&T introduced its formal telework policy; the program developed almost on its own from there. In other words, the benefits to the employee, company and community drove telework forward, as opposed to formal incentives and goals. Today, we find that over half of our managers (56%) telework at least one day a month, over a quarter (27%) of our managers telework one day or more per week, and 11% of our managers telework 100% of the time in a 'Virtual Office'."

AT&T has the luxury that a great deal of its work naturally falls into the telecommutable category, and it is certainly ideally placed when it comes to understanding the tools and infrastructure necessary. It may nonetheless come as a surprise to see the extent to which the company considers its work to be suitable to the remote approach:

"In our case (except for contractual obligations with represented employees) we assume all employees are eligible to telework until proven otherwise. We do not start with a universe of jobs, and then segregate out the teleworkable ones; we begin by assuming all jobs are teleworkable. Nor do we identify different locations (e.g. telecenters vs. homes) for different types of work. We believe that location is irrelevant, given the right technology; the work comes to the worker, no matter where she or he is."

Which is not to say that AT&T has confused work that *can* be done remotely with work which *should* be done remotely. That decision is still taken at a local level in consultation with managers and individual staff:

"AT&T places the actual telework participation decision (along with many other tactical decisions such as specific equipment provided) into the hands of the local manager and the proposed teleworker. These two are in the best position to understand the unique job and environment involved, and manage the culture change involved with successful implementation of telework. They fill out a 'teleworker's agreement' and there are no further approvals required. This empowered, flexible approach allows an individual employee to work at home as needed, when needed, to meet the competing demands of work, family, and society. What we have done is work to eliminate the structural barriers to telework ... programs which require teleworker approval by Vice Presidents have less participation than programs which require teleworker approval by direct managers."

As well as identifying the structural barriers to telework, AT&T has proved unusually sensitive to the cultural barriers involved. In response to those the company has embarked on a continuous round of internal marketing, "selling" the idea of telework on the basis of business and personal benefits. Those benefits are substantial – the company estimates that it saves $25mn a year in real estate alone, but that's just the tip of the iceberg:

"Data indicate that teleworking enhances productivity, both because teleworkers report being more productive per unit time, and because the teleworker has available the previously non-productive commute time. For example, when asked about perceived productive work hours (when tasks are accomplished), office workers reported 6.2 productive hours in an 8 hour day, compared to the teleworker-reported 7.5 hours in an 8 hour day. Over three-quarters (77%) of all teleworkers reported higher productivity at home while only 6% reported higher productivity in the office. Seven-in-ten managers (72%) report being more productive when working from home. Only 5% of managers report higher productivity when working from the office. We calculate that this increased productivity of our teleworkers is worth about $100M per year."

That's aside from less easily quantified benefits such as staff recruitment and retention rates:

"Among the AT&T teleworkers who have been offered other jobs, about two-thirds (67%) reported that giving up an 'AT&T telework environment' was a factor in their decision to remain with the company. And, in the competitive market for high tech employees, firms are finding that it is the companies with more non-traditional work environments that are the most successful in recruiting the knowledge worker."

As well as benefits to the company there are considerable individual benefits for the worker:

"77% of our employees who work from home reported much greater satisfaction with their current career responsibilities than before teleworking, while 84% said the same of their personal/family lives. Equally as interesting, not just the teleworker but their families also report enhanced quality of life: 81% of AT&T teleworkers reported their family members viewed the arrangements as positive, while only 3% reported negative feelings from other members of their households and 16% reported neutral opinions."

Time-line

» **Late 1980s**: company starts looking into telecommuting as a means of meeting the provisions of the federal Clean Air Act, one objective of which was to reduce air pollution produced by automobiles.

» **1989**: test project started in Los Angeles.

» **1990**: test project expanded to Phoenix, Arizona. After six months an analysis of the results led to realization of benefits for company and worker alike and the project was expanded. Time spent developing an overall implementation plan and employee education procedures, the educational material development being finished in mid-1994.

» **1994, September 20**: the company announced a company-wide Employee Telecommute Day. Even the then chairman, Robert Allen, telecommuted from home.

» **1998**: by now, of the 126,000 employees, over 30,000 (including half of the managerial and professional staff) telecommuted regularly.

» **2001, March 23**: AT&T's testimony to Congress reports that 56% of managers telework at least one day a month, 27% of managers telework one day or more per week, and 11% of managers telework 100% of the time in a "Virtual Office."

Facts and figures

Over the last several years, AT&T has developed Alternative Officing, a comprehensive program that currently allows 30,000 employees nationally to telecommute on a regular basis from home. This project is particularly interesting because it includes a rigorous cost/benefit analysis of their North Central New Jersey site. AT&T conducted a five-year study of 600 telecommuters and reached the following conclusions.

» The most substantial savings were in reduced real estate costs. By allowing employees to telecommute, AT&T was able to close an entire office complex. Annual real estate savings: $6,333,124.

» In addition to hard cost-savings, there were substantial productivity gains. AT&T, based on employee interviews, estimates a conservative gain of 2.5 hours per employee per week in time worked. Annual gain due to increased productivity: $5,112,841.

» Also, employees state almost without exception that they were able to be more productive during the hours they worked, due primarily to fewer interruptions. Annual gain due to increased efficiency: $3,127,617.

» There were, of course, start-up costs associated with setting up employees to work at home. Office alterations averaged $3000 per employee and computer/phone installations averaged $4000 per employee. These costs were depreciated over five years and $1250 per employee per year was added for phone, fax, copy, and postage bills. Annual costs: $3,205,507.

In short:

Real estate savings $6,333,124
Productivity gains (hour) $5,112,841
Productivity gains (efficiency) $3,127,617
Total $14,573,582
Less costs ($3,205,507)
Net annual gain $11,368,075

KEY LEARNING POINTS

» Arguably the standard-bearer for corporate telework, AT&T's zeal has to be seen in the light of its commercial interests in encouraging others to do likewise, but it undoubtedly makes a good argument for its case through detailed reporting of the statistics and the savings. That it does so is proof positive of the importance of measuring (see Chapter 10) and tracking satisfaction levels and financial savings alike.

» It's also key that, while much of AT&T's success is measurable in dollars saved, this is achieved so by realization that teleworking is a cultural more than a technological issue. As Dr Allenby put it when addressing Congress: "Part of the reason for AT&T's dramatic levels of telework is our management approach. We believe that telework should not be a separate and distinct area of the business. Instead, telework should be integrated into the business ... almost every existing organization plays a role in terms of policies, processes, and procedures within the existing business functions."

> • Managing the managers (see Chapter 10) has unlocked the teleworking door and released the capabilities of the company as a result.

SYSTEMATIC RESISTANCE? – THE JAPANESE EXPERIENCE

Japan remains the proof absolute that teleworking is more a cultural than a technological issue, but that does not mean that Japanese companies are not prepared to investigate telework, just that the challenges are very different.

The Japanese management approach, with its emphasis on very visible management and hierarchy, is not the most natural spawning ground for remote working practices. Wendy A. Spinks of the Science University of Tokyo points out that:

"While the innovative nature of Japanese work practices on the manufacturing shop floor is relatively well-documented (for example, Total Quality Management, kaizen and just-in-time distribution), white-collar work practices in office-based settings have remained largely unchanged throughout Japan's high growth period. The prolonged recession and increasingly swift penetration of information technology in the 1990s, however, are causing corporate Japan to seriously rethink its post-war patterns of white-collar employment and organization ... part of this corporate reassessment involves experimenting with flexible work arrangements."

Spinks cites the example of the Kansai Electric Power Company (KEPCO), which supplies electricity to Osaka, Kyoto, and Nara. As part of its plan for a new head office KEPCO opted to look into alternative facilities including home/alternative offices and mobile work patterns for 100 employees. The fact that it has recently purchased a telco gives it good infrastructure skills and puts it in a position to learn more about offering telco services in the process. Forthcoming deregulation in the industry provides further incentive to explore flexible and cost-efficient practices.

The result was a three-phase, three-year pilot launched back in July 1998. Whilst there is no intention of full-time teleworking in the pilot scheme, all teleworkers are expected to work at least one day a week. In a move that would raise eyebrows amongst Western teleworkers, all of the rules about work times and the length of work-breaks still apply to teleworkers, who must clock on and off by e-mail. The first phase saw 68 workers embark on this voyage of discovery, a number that has since risen to 120 and seen their ranks swell by a further 400 mobile workers using IT to report back to headquarters. For the teleworkers KEPCO introduced telework centers into corporate housing (it is still normal for Japanese corporations to provide housing for employees), an important factor in its success for reasons that Spinks spells out:

"Home offices are often disliked because of the difficulty in demar-cating private and work life, especially in typically small and confined Japanese urban housing. Telework centers offer a more controlled climate, which appeals to managers, but cost a lot to establish. They also do not offer the same commute reductions as home-based working. In that sense, offering a teleworking facility in corporate housing, which many of Japan's larger companies still provide, would seem to offer the best of both worlds: proximity to home but not actually at home."

To date the pilot appears to have proved an unexpected success. Predictably there have been attitude problems and the lack of under-standing displayed by non-teleworkers is cited as a hurdle to overcome. Nonetheless, Spinks reports that:

"The majority of teleworkers, supervisors and co-workers acknowl-edged greater productivity, the most frequently cited increase by all three groups being 10%. More than half of all three groups also cited greater overall organizational efficiency due to the introduction of telework."

While European and American teleworkers would be horrified to find that they had to comply with rigid rules regarding attendance at the keyboard, their Japanese equivalents seem to have found the experience liberating:

"Some 90% of teleworkers and their supervisors found telework to have fostered greater worker autonomy. More than 70% of the teleworkers thought telework had led them to reassess how they went about their work."

With subsequent benefits for both home and corporate life:

"More than 70% of both teleworkers and supervisors cited a better balance between work and home life for the teleworkers, while more than 70% of all three groups believed the telework pilot had enhanced the company's image at large."

Time-line

» **1997**: KEPCO begins to consider a pilot scheme to investigate the benefits of telework.
» **1998, July**: first phase of project begins and actual telework begins, largely from telecenters established in corporate supplied housing.
» **1999, July**: second phase sees original number of 68 workers swell to 120.
» **1999**: mobile working introduced, affecting some 400 workers.
» **2000**: number of teleworkers increased to 200, frequency of work increased from one day a week to two or more.

KEY LEARNING POINT
» While the case makes it clear that there are still cultural issues for telework in Japan, and a flexible worker in the US or UK would be appalled at being bound to the same strict work hours as an office worker, the pilot has shown that teleworking can show benefits even within the confines of Japanese management practice. By Western standards, however, this is still a top-down solution to something that is best managed at local level (see AT&T above). Most disquieting is the feedback about lack of understanding from those involved and it is tempting to suspect that the biggest task ahead of Japanese corporations will be that of internal marketing for the new practice.

REMOTE WORKING FOR ROAD WARRIORS – THE NEWSGEAR EXAMPLE

One of the earliest and most triumphant demonstrations of Bell's telephone was the transmission of a speech from Salem to the *Boston Globe* newspaper, which splashed the fact across its pages with the words "this special despatch of the *Globe* has been transmitted by telephone in the presence of twenty people, who have thus been witnesses to a feat never before attempted – the sending of news over the space of sixteen miles [about 25km] by the human voice."

The technology has changed since that day, but the importance of remote work and communications to the news industry most certainly hasn't. The news reporter is still the road warrior *par excellence*, a knowledge-worker in the field who becomes worthless to the organization if they are unable to report back and transfer the results of their work. The newspaper industry has an international organization called Ifra (www.ifra.com) based in Darmstadt, Germany, which acts as a knowledge pool for newspapers all over the world. One of its areas of expertise is the equipment needed in the field, and for the last three years it has run a project called NewsGear in which it field-tests the available technology for the reporter. In charge of the project is Kerry Northrup, an award-winning career journalist with extensive newsroom management experience and expertise in editorial technologies. Northrup started his professional newspaper career as a copy-editor with the *St Petersburg Times* in Florida, and spent more than 15 years as a reporter and editor at newspapers in South Carolina, Indiana, Florida, New Hampshire, and Vermont, so his interest in the subject goes beyond a simple love of gadgets.

The purpose of this rolling project is to equip a reporter so that one person can supply not just news, but pictures, sound, and even video, all of which can be transmitted back to the newsroom from the field. All the equipment has to fit into a hard-shell briefcase acceptable as hand luggage on an airline and able to be slipped under an airline seat. Northrup has an enviable role in the project – he gets to be guinea pig for the best. Recommendations come in from member newspapers of the group all over the world but it's Northrup who probably has the plum role as guinea pig for the best technologies. Since his own job involves extensive travel, meeting, and consulting with newspapers around the globe, he is relatively well placed to judge the strengths and weaknesses of the various products. Every year the NewsGear line-up is revised as new devices come to light, but also as new needs are reported by newspapers. Since newspapers increasingly have their own Websites, that role goes beyond the standard text and spreadsheet capability of many road workers, and includes the need for multimedia on the move.

At Ifra Expo 2001, the annual meeting of media minds in Amsterdam, Kerry Northrup demonstrated the full NewsGear line-up as follows.

The Palm Vx hand-held computer from Palm Computing Inc. is a device that it is small enough to slip into a shirt pocket, but is useful for scribbling notes with its pen stylus and hand-writing recognition language (Graffiti). Because most reporters can type faster than they can use Graffiti, however, the Palm's function-ality is extended by the addition of the Palm Portable Keyboard. A full-sized QWERTY keyboard, it folds up into a package no bigger than the Palm itself and can thus provide reporters with all they need to write copy, without lugging a portable computer to the scene. Even more remarkable is the addition of the Kodak PalmPix Camera. The PalmPix clips onto the Palm Pilot and allows it to take 24-bit color 480×640 resolution images. Whilst that doesn't provide newspaper-quality reproduction, the resulting images are certainly adequate for the Internet and the portability of the whole system makes it a true anytime/anywhere solution suitable for the most spontaneous of reports.

Northrup also demonstrated a clip-on GPS module and Minstrel wireless modem for the Palm, which meant that not only could the reporter file the resulting copy and images from the field but that they would also be accompanied by a precise record of the event's time and location. On a slightly more mundane note the same technology has been used by a PR company in the UK to ensure that public relations executives can recognize journalists that they are expected to meet up with at train stations and airports. The camera/PDA combination is used to build up a database of pictures of the journalists. After that, any PR executive waiting at an airport can request and receive a photograph of the person they're supposed to be meeting via a PDA equipped with a wireless modem, or hooked up to their mobile phone.

Text is not the last word any more when it comes to data capture for a newspaper, and the need for high quality pictures for print goes beyond the capability of most PDA cameras. As a result, the other focus of the NewsGear presentation was on multimedia in the form of a Sony Mavica MVC CD1000 digital camera that records directly onto an 18cm CD. The write-once CD is then a permanent archive for the paper.

Canon's digital motion camera, the Elura2 MC, was also selected as "one of the best of the crop of digital video cameras" but one over which Northrup voices a key reservation: "Really we're all waiting for a DV camera with high enough resolution to take stills from that are good enough for publishing in a newspaper. The highest DV cameras now have one million pixels, and you need two million to get A4 newsprint quality." As a stopgap the Elura functions in both video and high-resolution still-photograph modes.

Another piece of Sony kit, the ICD-MS1 voice recorder, was also chosen for its very high quality sound. "It's possible to record sound bites for the Web," notes Northrup, "but also good enough to take sound files and run them through Dragon Natural Speaking to convert it to text files. It also had to use portable media so you can send the media into the newsroom and the Sony Memory Stick media used has a media capacity of up to 128 megabytes. Plus it has the battery life necessary to make it through a two to three hour meeting."

The purpose of Dragon Natural Speaking is to convert recorded text to speech, so that a lengthy speech can be stored as text and then searched for key words when a journalist is sifting through for remarks relevant to the article being worked on. It's an increasingly common practice, largely thanks to the advent of the MiniDisc. As well as providing a lightweight alternative to the Walkman on dull journeys, the pocket MiniDisc player/recorders mean that many reporters can now record 90 minutes (per disc) of speech in a digital format that can then be computer processed. While the Palm is the solution for the newsroom in the pocket, the processing power required to use a tool like Dragon Natural Speaking (speech to text conversion) means that the NewsGear kit does also include a traditional portable computer. On the basis of weight to power and price, NewsGear selected the IBM ThinkPad T20 to fulfill that role. The laptop can also be used to download and edit the sound and video files captured with the

Sony and Canon equipment. Basic editing, such as filtering unwanted noise out of sound files, cropping pictures, or cutting video files to length, can all be performed on the laptop but since these are less immediate activities, the way Ifra expects the system to develop is for the recording device and Palm to accompany the reporter while the laptop waits back in the hotel room, ready for less urgent work.

That idea of a laptop being used in conjunction with a lightweight partner machine is also catching on in other industries, particularly as devices are produced to run Windows CE (the slimmed down version of Microsoft's operating system). So, for example, it is not unusual now for a road warrior to have the familiar laptop as a base station, but to pocket a lightweight CE device (such as a Compaq Aero) for short trips where all that's needed is basic spreadsheeting, text, and e-mail.

Last, but not least, among the NewsGear findings is that the entire collection of kit mentioned above was available for around $7000. Not only is that not extortionate when you consider what it includes, but compared to previous NewsGear line-ups it shows a year-on-year decrease in cost, despite the leaps and bounds in the technology itself.

KEY LEARNING POINT

» The main thing that the road warrior will find interesting about the NewsGear findings is not only the way in which sophisticated multimedia, including digital video and sound, have come within reach of the individual on the move, but that the price of managing that multimedia is coming down as dramatically as the quality is going up. Even for those with no interest whatsoever in sound and vision there is a lot to learn from the two-tier approach, whereby the laptop is left at base where possible, and a much more portable device taken out for fieldwork.

Key Concepts and
Thinkers

A glossary of key concepts, from "adhocracy" to "virtual company,"
and a look at some of the principal proponents of remote working.

KEY CONCEPTS

Adhocracy

Coined by Alvin Toffler in *Future Shock* (1970), the adhocracy is defined as a non-bureaucratic networked organization. "This form is already common in organizations such as law firms, consulting companies, and research universities. Such organizations and institutions must continually readjust to a changing array of projects, each requiring somewhat different combinations of skills and other resources. These organizations depend on many rapidly shifting project teams and much lateral communication among these relatively autonomous, entrepreneurial groups." (*Scientific American*, Sept. 1991, p.133.)

The key to a useful adhocracy is partly the area of knowledge management, a hot topic in software development and management. At its lowest level knowledge management is little more than an efficient archive and retrieval system for a company's knowledge of itself. Not just the documents and internal information that are compiled on the intranet, but such knowledge as personal specialities. More sophisticated systems such as IBM's Raven project track all the information movement within a company and automatically pick out the specialists. When another employee or project group has a query or task where a speciality applies then the system puts the two together (although whether they actually collaborate remains down to the individuals involved). The biggest challenge for most companies in encouraging adhocracies remains the familiar management moan that few companies really know what they know, a fact that also leads to time-wasting duplication of tasks, particularly in large organizations.

Concentrative teleworking

This is a term explained by the ETO (European Telework Online) which chooses to typify approaches such as telecottaging and telecenters as "distributed" teleworking – where work that previously would have been done at a central office is distributed to homes, telecenters, etc. The ETO (www.eto.org.uk) points out that the reverse is also possible:

"The technology also enables the reverse process, and in some types of work this can be very effective. An example of concentrative telework was provided by Dell, who brought together customer support operations from several European countries and concentrated them in centres in Ireland and the UK. American Express has taken a similar route."

Evanescent organization

As Jack Nilles explains in his article "What's an evanescent organization – and why should I care?" an evanescent organization is a term he himself coined in the late 70s:

". . . to describe the kind of organization that is strictly ad hoc: it vanishes. That is, it forms in response to a specific challenge, addresses the challenge and then evaporates once the issues have been resolved. This is not to say that the people in the organization are vaporized – they simply form other combinations in response to changing conditions."

"A good example of this is an organization I heard about in 1992, in Sophia Antipolis, France. One of the participants in the conference was a fellow who phoned in his story (clearly a teleworker). He ran a research organization that comprised himself, as the project leader, and a varying cast of researchers from around the world. His technique was quite simple. He spent several hours daily surfing the Internet and building a database of who was doing what research around the world. He also tracked those who had specific research needs. When searches of his database of researchers matched expressed corporate or government research needs, he acted as broker and project manager to connect the concerned parties, negotiate the terms, and complete the needed research task. After a project is completed, the researchers and the company employing them go their several ways, leaving only the core individual of this evanescent organization. All of this from a small village in the Maritime Alps."

"Obviously, this individual is a quintessential entrepreneur. Not all of us are. But, in this time of disemployment euphemisms like down- and right-sizing, it may be worth your while to consider some of the alternatives to traditional organization forms. You don't necessarily have to throw away your experience and expertise just because your local employer doesn't want it at the moment. Your future employer(s) could be anywhere."

Evanescent organizations can be within or without a company, and their creation has been helped by online virtual meeting-places and software that can be set up to provide private Web-based environments complete with scheduling, whiteboarding, brainstorming sessions and document storage. These offices, such as the Lotus product SamePlace, or eRoom (see Chapter 9) can be set up for a strictly limited period of time and so created and then scrapped on a project-by-project basis.

As the tools to create evanescent organizations have become more common, and work practices have continued to evolve, so Jack Nilles has since added a couple more terms to the remote working glossary.

Groupware

The term groupware was coined to categorize the original Notes software from Lotus, which combined the elements of chat rooms, messaging, and schedulers (amongst others) into one package. Groupware tools came of age with the availability of local- and wide-area networks which made it possible for individuals to go from working in isolation to working together in groups, whether real-time or not. The Website Usability First (www.usabilityfirst.com) defines groupware as "any type of software designed for groups and for communication, including e-mail, videoconferencing, workflow, chat, and collaborative editing systems."

This technology may be used to communicate, co-operate, co-ordinate, solve problems, compete, or negotiate. While traditional technologies such as the telephone qualify as groupware, the term is ordinarily used to refer to a specific class of technologies relying on modern computer networks, such as e-mail, newsgroups, videophones, or chat.

Groupware technologies are typically categorized along two primary dimensions: whether users of the groupware are working together at the same time ("real-time" or "synchronous" groupware) or different times ("asynchronous" groupware); and whether users are working together in the same place ("collocated" or "face-to-face") or in different places ("non-collocated" or "distance").

Network organizations/distributed organizations

Just as the growth of the Internet has added weight to the claim that the network is the computer, so the growth of flexible work practices is making it true that the network is now the organization. By providing a means for collaboration between specialists who are not in the same location, or even in the same company, it is possible to maximize the use of available knowledge and talent. Companies and organizations then form in which the connection between workers is not the workplace, or even the employer, but the task at hand and the technology that enables them to work together to complete it. Of these organizations Jack Nilles notes that:

> "These are also known as distributed organizations. The term can refer to distributed branches or divisions of a single firm or a well-defined consortium of co-operating firms. All of them use ICT as an important means of efficient communication among the distributed parts. A major characteristic of a network organization is that the separate nodes in the network operate relatively autonomously, although governed by the overall policies, business rules, and procedures of the network as a whole."

Open-collar workers

As opposed to blue- or white-collar workers, open-collar workers are those who work at home or telecommute. Less charitable commentators have been known to point out that even an open collar would often represent a dress-up day for many home workers.

Road warriors

A glamorous term for an increasingly mundane phenomenon, the road warrior is simply the worker on the move, usually identifiable in trains and airport lounges by the mobile phone and laptop computer. The biggest change in the road warrior's development is that increasing data speeds for mobile phones (see Chapter 6) and the impending release of permanently-on, high-bandwidth mobile telephony means that being on the road may no longer mean intermittent connection to the office. Instead the road warrior and the telecenter or home-worker are likely to become increasingly similar in the eyes of the organization in terms of ease of contact and potential for collaboration.

As the sheer quantity of technology available to the mobile worker has grown (mobile phone, PDA, GPS, Webcam, etc.), so the road warrior term has become ever more appropriate with itinerant executives tooling-up with hardware before taking to the field in a manner curiously reminiscent of Stallone or Schwarzenegger.

Road warriors are also known as nomadic teleworkers.

Satellite offices

A satellite office is much like a telecottage but with the difference that where most telecottages are set up to be shared by a number of knowledge workers, who often have only their location in common, a satellite office is usually owned only by one company. In order to benefit from a pool of talent that cannot easily commute to the established office the company sets up a satellite nearer its workers. The satellite is linked to the mother office by the technology necessary for tele-cooperation and workers then commute to the site that suits them best.

Telecenters

In some cases the satellite office and the telecenter are one and the same and the term can be used interchangeably. Where they differ, however, is that a telecenter doesn't have to be for the benefit of a single company. It may even be set up as a separate commercial entity renting space and facilities to a wide variety of remote workers.

Tele-cooperation

Tele-cooperation simply means that a group of physically remote people come together to work on a common task. It doesn't necessarily mean that there is any mobile working involved, or indeed any break from the nine-to-five norm, since tele-cooperation could simply mean that branch offices are linked up via the company network to collaborate on a project. In its more extreme forms, however, it can entail individual workers in different continents and time zones passing work backwards and forwards, for example programmers in Bangalore working through the US night-time to finish off code for colleagues in Boston. Tele-cooperation can be for a limited period, using temporary virtual workspaces on the Net (see the evanescent organization, above) or it can be a regular practice, in which case the most common toolset used to link fellow workers is called groupware (see above).

Telecottages

Best known from its use in Alvin Toffler's *The Third Wave*, in which the futurist envisaged electronic cottages complete with computers that would allow the workforce to work from home. The term "telecottage" is widely accepted to be a Scandinavian one but there is disagreement as to whether it came from Denmark or the Swedish term "telestuga." It became popular in the UK in the 80s thanks to ACRE (Action with Rural Communities in England). A reference to the idea of a cottage industry, the term is actually quite confusing since it doesn't mean home-work but is usually used to mean small telecenters located in rural areas, particularly in the UK where ACRE promoted the idea of rural regeneration by setting up office areas with the requisite technology for remote working. Even the TCA (Telecentre Association), the UK's leading organization supporting and promoting teleworking, uses the terms telecenter and telecottage pretty much interchangeably. Because of its rural association, the term telecottage is more often used for remote areas where a community sets up a location with computers and telecommunications facilities to help local business, community groups, and individuals. Some feel that the associations of "cottage" are too parochial, however, and prefer the term telecenter no matter how rural or remote the location may be.

Televillage

Again, the most helpful definition of this idea comes from the ETO Website (www.eto.org.uk/faq), which defines a televillage as:

> "an extension of the telecottage and is very much about lifestyles and preferences. The idea is to develop a whole community that's highly geared to the future work and lifestyles environment of the networked economy – the whole village is 'wired' and each home is fully equipped with an internal network connected to the village network and through broadband communications to the 'global village'..."

> "A televillage is being developed near Crickhowell in Wales and the idea is being discussed in other environmentally attractive areas such as the Highlands and Islands region of Scotland. Several such projects are at various stages of development in North America."

Teleworking

As Gil Gordon, a celebrated remote working consultant, explains:

> "The term 'telework' tends to be used more in Europe and some other countries, while 'telecommuting' is used more in the US. Some people prefer the word 'telework' because it's a more accurate description of the concept – the 'tele' prefix means 'distance,' so 'telework' means 'work at a distance.' The telework advocates also believe that 'telecommuting' has too strong a connotation about the commuting aspect, and that 'telework' is a broader and more inclusive term ... Whatever you choose to call it, the underlying concept is the same: decentralizing the office, and using different ways of bringing the work to the workers. It doesn't make much difference (to me, at least) what you call it – as long as you do it."

Virtual call-centers

The call-center, answering enquiries and complaints, has become a familiar part of the corporate structure, and an essential (if often expensive) one at that. Because call-center workers have no face-to-face contact with their clients, this was one of the first areas to benefit from remote working practices. At first the emphasis was on locating call-centers far from the parent company in areas where real estate was cheaper and a local pool of suitable talent existed. With a virtual call-center, however, there is no need to find a single area that supplies the necessary abilities (often a headache with less easily found skills). Instead the call-center workers may be scattered across a country in small satellite offices. They may even be individuals at home. They call up the centralized call-center server system to log on and the exchange then parcels out calls to whoever is appropriate wherever they are. The client has no idea where the worker is, and has no need to know. The growth of technologies such as Voice-over IP (see Chapter 6) has made it possible for a call-center worker to work from almost anywhere, the nearest phone being transformed into their own, complete with the speed-dial and memory options normally only associated with a fixed office phone.

Virtual company

"Like network organizations, this term had about as many definitions as there are definers. The most common version focuses on
the concept that the virtual organization is location-free. That is, it
may have no fixed place where there is a corporate headquarters.
Although it may have a postal address, URL, and central phone
number, the postal address may be a drop box somewhere, the
Website is monitored by the Webmaster, and the phone number
may just automatically forward calls to whomever is in charge of
the service desired. Virtual organizations are generally small since
size tends to force accumulation of property."

Jack Nilles

Virtual office

A virtual office can be another way of describing a virtual company
(see above) but is also applied to the software that enables users to
set up private collaboration space on the Web. These spaces include
messaging, scheduling, deadline and delivery date information for the
participants and often use instant chat or videoconferencing to enable
meetings. Virtual offices can also be electronic communication that
appears to have a physical location. So, for example, there are services
that give you a fax number in Japan even though you have no presence
there. The idea is that for Japanese clients it may be cheaper and more
acceptable to fax to what seems to be a Tokyo office than your real
office in Tooting, London, or Tucson, Arizona. In reality the fax is
never printed out in Tokyo but instantly sent as a bitmap image to your
e-mail account. Similarly it is possible to have an answering machine
that appears to be in Boston, Massachusetts, but actually works by
transmitting the messages, converted to text, to your mobile phone in
Boston, England.

KEY THINKERS

Gil Gordon

(www.gilgordon.com)

One of the best known telecommuting advocates, Gil Gordon,
became established in the early 80s as a consultant to public and

private sector ventures setting up telework projects. He published the *Telecommuting Review*, and was honored by ITAC in 1999 as "a globally known pioneer in fostering telecommuting and telework concepts. The Telework Hall of Fame Award, the highest honor bestowed by ITAC, is given to Gil for his sustained and lasting contributions toward creating well-planned and well-managed telework programs benefiting employers, employees, and society as a whole."

Jack Nilles

(www.jala.com)

A former engineer at NASA where he headed design teams for space vehicles, Nilles coined the terms telecommuting and teleworking in 1973 after research prompted by the simple, but loaded, point was put to him that we can send a man into space but we still suffer increasingly from traffic congestion. Commonly referred to as "the father of telecommuting/teleworking," he founded the management consulting firm, JALA International Inc., in 1980.

He is the author of five books, including *The Telecommunications-Transportation Tradeoff*, the original book on telecommuting, as well as *Making Telecommuting Happen*, published in 1994, and its sequel, *Managing Telework: Strategies for Managing the Virtual Workforce*, published in 1998. His influence has bridged the Atlantic thanks to his work for the European Commission reviewing the state of play and future possibilities for telework in Europe.

Alvin Toffler

Known best for the books *Future Shock, The Third Wave,* and *Powershift*, Alvin Toffler is both a respected social critic and one of the world's most popular futurists. He has long argued that remote and flexible working is the way forward for society and popularized the idea of telecottaging.

Resources

Extensive listings of Websites and books with relevant information.

ROAD WARRIOR SITES

3G portal

http://www.the3gportal.com

The place to go to check out the state of play in the next wave of mobile telephony.

Palm Pilot

http://www.palmpilot.org

Useful downloads, tips, hand-held news, and everything a Palm OS user could want to know about life on the move.

Kropla

http://www.kropla.com

Planning an international trip? Take a look at this site before you go, and print it off for use in an emergency. Kropla.com is simply the Web's most comprehensive listing of worldwide electrical and telephone information, including international dialing codes, electricity supply information, and a world phone guide. Everything you could want to know about getting online from a strange hotel room is to be found at http://www.kropla.com/phones.htm. Advice on everything from "tax impulse" signals (used to meter calls) interfering with your data, to basic wire-tapping to acoustic couplers, just about anything and everything you could need to know in order to hook up. With the data on this site you can get online from just about anywhere.

Road Warrior Outpost

http://www.warrior.com

Published by Road Warriors International, this site locates replacement computer parts for travelers with laptops – something that will be appreciated by anyone whose ageing machine looks set to outlive its current battery. Also features road warrior links and a free monthly *Road Warrior* e-mail newsletter.

FINDING A CYBERCAFÉ AT YOUR TARGET DESTINATION

Going to be out of the country/continent for a few days? You might want to take a portable and log on, but if all you want is to check your e-mail occasionally then a cybercafé may be all you need. There are books that list cybercafés, but these are rarely that extensive and inevitably date badly so that cafés have shut or moved even before publication. Try a dedicated cybercafé search engine instead.

cybercafe.com
http://www.cybercafe.com

Cybercafe.com is a search engine to help you find out where to go to log on before you arrive in that strange city.

This site currently contains a database of 4193 Internet cafés in 148 countries but new ones are added all the time and you can recommend ones you know. You can search by city or country name for a list of cafés found in that location, or click on the map below for quick access to regional listings. Listings include location (country, city, address), home page URL, and e-mail address.

cybercaptive.com
http://cybercaptive.com

Like cybercafe.com, cybercaptive.com is a search engine for finding those elusive public access points and one which claims (as of June 2001) database listings for 6739 verified cybercafés, public Internet access points, and kiosks in 167 countries.

FAMILY LIFE/WORKING MOTHER SITES

Families and Work Institute
http://www.familiesandwork.org

Families and Work Institute is a non-profit organization that concerns itself with the changing nature of work and family life. It's not specifically telework-based, but remote working is one of the recurrent themes amongst the reports and research into strategies that "foster mutually supportive connections among workplaces, families, and communities."

Telecommuting – the convergence of work, home, and family spheres
http://edie.cprost.sfu.ca/~chiklink/453home.html

A paper on the way in which telework will affect the spheres of work, home, family, and the role of women.

Working Moms' Refuge

http://www.momsrefuge.com/telecommute

Featuring articles on taming tension, the art of juggling family and telework, the role of dad and the problems for single mothers. Not always directly telework-related, but a thought provoking collection of resources about the social aspect of working from home.

Home Working Mom

http://www.homeworkingmom.com

Ostensibly oriented more towards the homebound mother looking for casual remote work than for the career telecommuter, Home Working Mom is the site for Mothers' Home Business Network, the first and largest national organization providing ideas, inspiration, and support for mothers who choose to work at home. A wide range of tips, from keeping children happy as you work, to tax issues, and accepting credit card orders.

Smart Eric

http://www.smarteric.com

Smart Eric claims to be the only Website that supports self-employed professionals and helps companies find freelances. The site includes advice on how to *Feng Shui* your desk, enhancing the well-being of your business, and adjusting to working at home.

GENERAL RESOURCES – PORTALS AND CASE STUDIES

Smart Valley telecommuting initiative

http://www.svi.org/PROJECTS/TCOMMUTE

The Smart Valley initiative was launched in 1993 and consisted of a pilot program with participants from several Silicon Valley firms. At that time it was the largest multi-company telecommuting study. A survey of the participants, their managers, and peers was conducted by Gemini Consulting Group and the results were published in October 1994. The survey was also used to calibrate a *Telecommuting Guide*, which is available in hard copy as well as an electronic version from Smart Valley's Website.

Case study and reports provide interesting background to more recent initiatives.

Washington State University telecommuting site

http://www.energy.wsu.edu/telework

WSU delights with this detailed, well-organized site. From training to tools to technical assistance, you can learn most of what you need to know about becoming a telecommuter, either for yourself or for your boss back at the office.

Although the most recent updates in terms of research and case studies date back to May 2000, the site is still of interest thanks to its collection of case studies as PDF files.

AT&T telework pages

http://www.att.com/telework

The standard-bearer for corporate teleworking, AT&T's telework site includes a calculator for working out potential telework savings, articles, and the full testimony to Congress in 2001 detailing AT&T's own case study. Not only one of the largest telework projects of its kind, the AT&T scheme is also one of the most detailed and the facts and figures are useful ammunition for telework advocates.

Working from anywhere (UK government)

http://www.ukonlineforbusiness.gov.uk/Advice/publications/teleworking/home.html

This site includes case studies, advice, and publications that can be applied for to help companies see how telework can benefit them in the UK.

Andrew Bibby's telework site

http://www.eclipse.co.uk/pens/bibby/telework.html

Andrew Bibby is an independent writer and journalist, who has written widely on the business and social implications of information and communication technologies. The site includes extracts from his books including *Making the Decision: is Telework Right For You?*, and a chapter originally published in *Home is Where the Office is: a Practical Handbook for Teleworking from Home* (Hodder, 1991).

Cyberworkers

http://www.cyberworkers.com

French telework portal.

Nothing But Net – American workers and the information economy

http://www.heldrich.rutgers.edu

This is a survey conducted by the Center for Survey Research and Analysis, University of Connecticut in Storrs, Connecticut, in which the university researchers conducted telephone interviews with 1005 adult workers in the 48 contiguous states. The results give a picture of attitudes, costs, and trends of teleworking in the US.

MITEL/MORI poll of UK workers' attitudes towards teleworking

http://www.mori.com/polls/2001/mitel.shtml

MITEL networks sponsored MORI to conduct this survey into the attitude of British office workers to the problems of their work and the potential of teleworking as a solution. The results suggest that a significant number are so convinced of the joys of telework that they would consider a pay cut in order to be allowed to do it.

CIO Magazine's wireless resource page

http://www.cio.com/forums/communications

A resource guide for all things wireless, including case studies past and present of companies including wireless as part of their communications system. Apart from the opinions and information, the site is worth a look just as a reminder of remote and wireless systems being implemented back in the 1980s before the Web was in place.

StartWright resources

http://www.startwright.com

A leading reference site for the information needs of information technology project managers and support staff traveling to, starting up, and working on remote or dispersed projects.

In particular, the links page at http://www.startwright.com/mobile. htm is a rich source of ideas and links to sources including most of the major European telework organizations as well as hardware and peripheral manufacturers for the would-be mobile worker.

Mobile Info

http://www.mobileinfo.com

Useful site specializing in wireless connectivity, whether by means of Bluetooth, WAP, or other up-and-coming technologies. Includes a case study section at http://mobileinfo.com/Case_Study/index.htm, which has a number of examples of good practice for mobile work, including UPS, IBM, Palm, and Synchrologic.

Escape Artist

http://www.escapeartist.com/tele/commute.htm

Escape Artist gives a very hands-on guide to getting away, including tests of products to enable Web meetings, videoconferencing, and Internet telephony, as well as expatriate resources and a list of embassies. This is a site for which remote working means not only working from another country or continent, but probably living there as well.

Gil Gordon

http://www.gilgordon.com

Gil Gordon is one of the best-known consultants on remote working in all its forms and his site, in addition to plugging his own books, contains a searchable database of telecommuting and telework resources from around the world, including books, articles, sites, and conferences.

TELECOMMUTING ORGANIZATIONS

International Telework Association & Council (ITAC)

http://www.telecommute.org

ITAC's mission statement is that it drives the growth and success of work independent of location. ITAC exists to study, develop, and recommend tools, techniques, and processes that promote the benefits of telework. It is also one of the more authoritative sites when it comes to documenting the growth and development of telework in the US.

European Telework Online (ETO)

http://www.eto.org.uk

Portal site for teleworking and telecommuting, includes helpful definitions of teletrade and tele-cooperation. The FAQ of terms is one of the clearest available and can be found at www.eto.org.uk/faq

Telecentre Association (UK)

http://www.tca.org.uk/home.htm

The TCA is Europe's largest organization dedicated to the promotion of teleworking with over 2000 individual and corporate members. The TCA provides advice on how to approach teleworking, information on technology, examples of how other people progress, and information about work opportunities. In the bi-monthly magazine, *Teleworker*, and in a weekly electronic bulletin, the TCA sends out updates and information about full-time and temporary telework opportunities.

InnoVisions Canada – the Canadian Telework Association

http://www.ivc.ca

This site represents a tie-up between InnoVisions, a telework consultancy, and the Canadian Telework Association, a non-profit-making association dedicated to promoting telework. Telework, taxes, cost savings, and of course details of the Canadian teleworking scene and conferences being held there are included.

In the telework news archives (http://www.ivc.ca/newsarchives7. htm) is a truly compelling collection of links to articles from far and wide about the implications and practice of remote working. Articles are mainly North American oriented but the scope of the site makes it of interest to the telework-curious wherever they hail from.

Japan Telework Association

http://www.japan-telework.or.jp/english/english_index.html

Reports, projects, and case studies in progress from the Land of the Rising Sun, including a Japanese Telework population survey, a survey on the actual conditions of the enterprises which practice telework, and studies requested by the ministries and local government offices.

Home Office Computing magazine

http://www.hocmag.net

For the remote worker in the home office with the usual mix of articles, opinions, and product reviews but also a strong emphasis on (and a section dedicated to) the idea of community. Written by others from their home offices it is an interesting forum for the practicalities of home-working.

June Langhoff's Telecommuting Resource Center

http://www.langhoff.com

June Langhoff describes herself as a televangelist, promoting telecommuting and other remote work styles instead of religion. An author, senior editor at *Telecommute* magazine, and of course a teleworker, her site is an agreeable mix of humor, light-heartedness, and healthy tips for working. Amongst other tools on site are details of how to prepare a cost/benefit analysis to convince your company to allow telecommuting, and links to statistics about the effects of remote working on productivity and morale.

Sociology Department, University of Amsterdam

http://www.pscw.uva.nl/sociosite/TOPICS/Telework.html

One of the most exhaustive reading and resource lists available for teleworking available on the Net. Articles and resources from 25 countries with information on the experts and the state of play from Israel to India.

You Can Work From Anywhere

http://www.youcanworkfromanywhere.com/index.html

A great site with upbeat articles on life on the road and at home with tips on online meetings and virtual offices. Also contains a useful collection of statistics on cost savings, trends, and productivity issues of working away from the office and includes *Road Work*, the free e-zine for the road warrior.

Flexibility – resources for flexible work

http://www.flexibility.co.uk/index.htm

Flexible working conferences, technologies for working anywhere, and perhaps best of all "12 ways to screw up a flexible work project" – Flexibility is a forum for discussion about the key issues of flexible working.

TECHNOLOGY AND TOOLS FOR REMOTE WORKERS

InfoTooth – Bluetooth Information Center

http://palowireless.com/infotooth

Friendly and remarkably jargon-free, this is a good first port of call for anyone curious about the possibilities of Bluetooth wireless technology. Includes articles and links with backgrounders, technical information, and state of play reports.

Enterasys VPN resource center

http://www.enterasys.com/technologies/vpn

While Enterasys Networks, as a provider of VPN systems, clearly has its own agenda, this page is a useful source of information about the benefits of VPN, and even includes some unusual features such as a VPN calculator (http://www.enterasys.com/aurorean/vpn_calculator/vpncalculator.html) which allows you to enter your company details and estimate how much money you could save by using VPN to link up to remote workers compared to, say, using 800 numbers for them to dial up.

Mobile Computing

http://www.mobilecomputing.com

This site is a great resource for all things hardware and software to do with getting out of the office. Whether it's buying a hand-held, choosing a digital camera, tips for world travellers or "how stuff works," Mobile Computing has the answers.

eRoom.net

http://www.eroom.net

eRoom is a product for organizing remote project teams, providing a virtual room, document sharing, scheduling, and threaded discussion groups. A template approach makes it simple to set such regular features as delivery dates, task "owners," and status reporting, and it links up to Microsoft Outlook to ensure that the group's deadlines and personal "to do" lists synch-up.

MagicalDesk

http://www.magicaldesk.com

A simple solution for retrieving mail from your company account whilst on the move as well as organizing group tasks. MagicalDesk is championed by Macintosh users since it is one of the few remote worker tools that has a purely Macintosh product – iMagicalDesk.

BOOKS

http://mobileinfo.com/Education/books.htm offers limited reviews of a number of books on wireless and mobile computing, as well as a listing of titles available on VPNs.

Still the star buy at the European Telework Organization is *Managing Telework* by Jack Nilles (John Wiley & Sons, 1998).

Those preferring to find a UK rather than a US take on telecommuting may want to look at the works of Ursula Huws, including *Telework: Towards the Elusive Office* by Ursula Huws, Werner B. Korte Simon Robinson (Chichester, John Wiley & Sons, 1989; paperback 1990).

More international perspectives can be explored courtesy of *Teleworking: International Perspectives* (paperback) by Paul J. Jackson and Jos M. van der Wielen (Routledge, 1998).

The following represents a selection of books aimed at the office refugee, taken from the selection at Escape Artist (http://www.escape-artist.com/books6/telcom.htm):

» *Virtual Office Survival Handbook: What Telecommuters & Entrepreneurs Need to Succeed in Today's Nontraditional Workplace*, by Alice Bredin (John Wiley & Sons, 1996);
» *Telecommute! Go to Work Without Leaving Home*, by Lisa Angowski Rogak Shaw (John Wiley & Sons, 1996); and
» *Digital Nomad*, by Tsugio Makimoto & David Manners (John Wiley & Sons, 1997).

Ten Steps for Making Flexible and Virtual Working Work

A step-by-step checklist of the hows and whys of ensuring remote working is both appropriate to the task and successfully implemented.

1. ANALYSIS

Before anything else it is important to take a look at the nature of the company, its workers, and their work. Can that work be done remotely and, if so, will it be done better remotely?

Where work is largely knowledge-based there is always the possibility of doing it remotely but a look at the work process is as important as the end result. Is the process one of continual dialogue with others, or a question of taking on-board input and doing research before setting down to produce the final work? If the latter is the case, then many people will positively benefit from being able to sit down and work outside of the office with its multiple distractions. If, however, the work involves continuous consulting of others, then it may make it more stressful to force people to exchange phone calls for meetings. It's worth considering whether the job can be broken down into recognizable steps or milestones that are compatible with different work environments.

Very few jobs lend themselves to full-time telework, but in an information economy there are equally few that couldn't benefit from one or two days a week away from the office. As ITAC puts it:

"Telework isn't appropriate for every job. Some job activities don't lend themselves to telework. Organizations need to analyze the job activity, not the job title, to determine suitability to telework. The key is to find jobs with at least a portion of the work that can be done, as well or better, away from the office – taking advantage of technology and getting away from the distractions and interruptions in the typical office."

ITAC then qualifies that by pointing out that:

"Even hands-on jobs such as fire-fighting can benefit from telework. For example, a fire chief in Fairfax County, Virginia, identified that report writing was one of his main activities, clearly a task that didn't have to be done at the firehouse. When he began to telework from his home office, his productivity shot up 20% because he produced reports more immediately, while he remembered the incident, and so more accurately."

In the course of analyzing whether the company's work is suitable for telework it must be remembered that the answer to that also depends on whether the company's workers are suited to telework. Many people need the discipline of working at set times in a shared workplace and find it hard to motivate themselves out of that routine. Others are immediately more productive when given the time and space to get on with their own work away from others. In its own telework recommendations AT&T makes the point that the key to good telework is trust:

> "Essentially, a 'good' employee or manager in the office is a good employee at home – a person's work ethic or results focus (as examples) do not change when she or he changes her or his desk. The key issue is really trust. If the manager trusts the employee to be getting work done even when she or he can't be seen, and if the employee trusts the manager to take her or his needs into account even when they aren't right outside the office door, then obviously there's a greater pool of 'eligible' teleworkers. If there's a lack of trust in either of these dimensions, then the eligible pool shrinks accordingly."

2. CONSULTING WITH STAFF

Surveys suggest that a significant number of office workers would be more than glad to telework at least once a week, but launching the policy as a *fait accompli* could have adverse effects on morale. Actively involving staff in the process is a key element in ensuring success and deciding on a strategy (telecottaging/telecenters?; one day/three days a week?; etc.) that will suit all concerned. Failure to consult can often lead to genuine benefits being perceived as negative points by the rumor-mill. It is easy for enthusiasm about savings in real estate to be understood as a sneaky step towards moving workers out to the middle of nowhere. Announcing to a department that from here on in they can work from home for two days a week could well be misconstrued as a step towards downsizing. A proper consultation process will include consideration of individual motivation for remote work, and potential problems. Someone with a small home and a large number of pre-school children, for example, might be better suited to a telecenter or satellite office approach than simply being sent home with a PC and a modem.

3. CONSULTING WITH THE IT DEPARTMENT

IT will most likely be expected to implement the technology needed for remote working, and even if they aren't (because the workers in question already have it in place) they should be actively involved in the consideration of what technology is in place if they are to "own" the problem of supporting it. The last thing a company needs is to lose productive time because a technical issue comes up with a home machine and everyone points at everyone else when it comes to fixing it. IT departments will have legitimate fears about servicing remote set-ups, and not just because of the distance involved in getting to them if on-site service is required. Letting them judge if the system in place will suit the task is a first step; establishing the protocols for support is the next. That might mean an escalating scale system whereby users are expected to first check an established FAQ list either on the Web or an intranet, then move up a support ladder if their needs are not answered.

Many companies insist on a standard set-up for remote machines and block the user from adding any further software. This can go a long way to reducing technical glitches but may not be appropriate where the remote machine is the user's own. Which is another point to think of when considering to what extent the company will pay to install the remote IT. One other popular solution is to pre-install machines with remote control software. This allows a remote engineer to take control of the keyboard and mouse over the phone and see the machine's display on their own screen. That means they can examine the computer as if they were sat at it themselves. Sorting out the remote hardware and software is only part of the problem of course, as even if all of that is deemed to be the remote worker's problem (as can happen in technical companies), the IT department is going to have to ensure that it is then possible to have remote access to the company network. This will mean configuring the firewall, setting up password gateways and monitoring for viruses. Security issues, including the risk of unauthorized access, must be addressed and proper procedure for intruder detection and damage limitation are highly advised.

4. ESTABLISHING THE SUPPORT GROUP

Setting up technical support is only part of the formula. Within a normal office environment a great many problems are resolved without recourse to the helpdesk – from asking your neighbor how the printer works to consulting the local alpha geek (the office expert) about encryption. It is important not to lose that support group by decentralizing the workforce. Creating an FAQ that everyone can access is a start. Providing incentives so that workers will then add to that wisdom is going one better. With groupware it may be possible to set up informal chat rooms to encourage discussion on a point and certainly there should be access to an e-mail directory so that workers can find each other and discuss things that they might not air in front of others. Remote workers need to exchange war stories in order to get perspectives on problems and solutions.

More advanced knowledge management systems can track who deals with which issues and identify them as topic experts, directing others to them regardless of where they happen to be located. The other issue of support is not strictly technical but somewhere in between business and social. Remote workers should be encouraged to look at how other people, including those from other companies, deal with such issues as juggling productivity and parenthood, or learning how and when to switch off – be that the TV or themselves. There are a number of online forums that deal with the subjects and swap tips (see the family life/working mother sites section of Chapter 9) – another strong argument for Web access for all teleworkers.

5. MANAGE THE MANAGERS

It's not just workers who run the risk of being alienated by being decentralized. Managers may find it hard to adapt to the new ways of working and a shift in their attitudes is key to the success of the project. Dr Carl van Horn and Duke Storen of the John J. Heldrich

Center for Workforce Development, at Rutgers, the State University of New Jersey, produced a study of the benefits of teleworking for the US Department of Labor. Amongst its conclusions was:

"The mindset of managers is widely regarded as a significant barrier to the growth of telework in the American economy. Firms that prefer to manage by seeing and checking on employees resist the idea of teleworking because of a 'fear of loss of control.' Human resource managers reported in a survey that the main obstacles to teleworking are the lack of supervision of employees, the absence of upper management support, and concerns about communicating with employees. For telework to grow more rapidly, managers will be required to emphasize results, rather than attendance. Interestingly, software exists to monitor workers' output based on the number of keystrokes performed, time on-line, and tasks completed. Despite fears that managers will lose control over low-wage workers if they are not in sight, the digital management tools are more effective in tracking the performance of this strata of workers than they are for monitoring mid-level and more senior staff whose work products are less quantifiable."

Their results can be found at http://www.heldrich.rutgers.edu.

6. WORK TO REALIZE THE BENEFITS

It's not enough to create telecenters or encourage home-working two days a week. In order for a remote working project to realize its potential, it must be pursued to the full. In particular, real estate savings won't happen if the original office remains untouched – instead the company will simply be paying out as before but now with the added problems of supporting a decentralized workforce. That doesn't necessarily mean doing away with the office, but it could mean smaller premises, or sharing with other companies in order to both reduce costs and increase possibilities of partnerships. Even where the idea is not to do away with or reduce the office space, it may still be worth rethinking the way it is laid out. If the emphasis has shifted away from it being a place where individuals come to work, it may no longer be appropriate to have it laid out that way. If offices are now primarily for meetings, or brainstorming and teamwork sessions, then that should shape the environment itself. If you are encouraging remote computing it may also be a good idea to make the office itself more "mobile-friendly" so that road warriors can log on when they come in. For that the company may want to look at adding ports or wireless Local Area Networks (LANs) to conference rooms or even cafeterias and deploy port replicators wherever people may want to connect to office-bound printers or scanners.

7. MEASURE THE RESULTS

In order to know if Step 6 is working you'll need to have measurement systems in place. That could mean anything from the expenditure on real estate to the reduction (hopefully) in unwanted absenteeism. Ensure you have feedback mechanisms, and that the results of feedback don't then disappear into the void. Gauging productivity is a process that varies from enterprise to enterprise but it is important to get a handle on how the performance of the organization is being affected by the introduction of remote working. Not only will that help convince the reluctant that it is a good idea but it will provide the necessary decision-making information to take the strategy further. Should you roll this out elsewhere? Or indeed should the whole show be canceled – there are examples of companies experimenting with telework only to go back to the conventional approach. Remote working is not a one-size-fits-all strategy after all.

8. MAINTAIN COMMUNICATION

The less workers are in the office, the more they need to make sure they are in the loop. Foreign correspondents, in many ways the precursors of the road warriors of today, used to be notorious for a paranoia and the feeling that they were the butt of office politics back home. The savings from travel are one of the premiums of remote working but it is possible to become too enamored with them and neglect the importance of face-to-face meetings. Just as the nature of the office may need to be rethought (see Step 6), so the nature of meetings may need to adapt to the need more for team-building than for information sharing. Communication can take a number of forms, from informal meetings to the less obvious strategies adopted by some companies. Sun Microsystems, for example, experimented with "talk radio" hosted by boss Scott McNealy, as a way of including workers in corporate changes. A major UK bank includes information downloaded to remote machines whenever they log on for their e-mail. That information is incorporated into their screensaver so that whenever the keyboard and mouse are idle for a pre-set period the screen comes alive with company announcements, tips, quotes, even jokes for the day.

9. CREATE PERSONAL WORKSPACE

In the case of individual remote workers, ensure that you have the workspace, both in terms of the physical space you need, and the understanding of colleagues and family. It is a common misconception that because you are at home, you must be at home to visitors. Likewise, it will often be presumed that you are free to do all the domestic chores, no matter how hard your work schedule. Maintaining a routine will be harder and for some that is a major problem, so schedule rigorously. A remote worker has more flexible time, and less time wasted commuting, but there are still only so many hours in the day. Setting goals and monitoring progress is crucial, all the more so for the fact that there is no supervisor looking over your shoulder.

10. BACKUPS AND FALLBACKS

In the case of the road warrior, think ahead and above all anticipate fallbacks. It is not enough to presume that your trusty laptop and its ageing internal modem will ensure hassle-free connectivity to the company. Think about how you will establish connections – are you counting on plugging in at a hotel or private home? And if so have you checked that you have the appropriate adapters? If your laptop dies, can you resort to your PDA? If you are used to relying on a wireless PDA, such as a Blueberry or a Palm VII, will it still work when abroad? Many wireless devices will not function outside of their home country simply because different countries reserve different frequencies for specific purposes including the military and police. If neither your PC nor your PDA works, will a cybercafé be there to come to the rescue? Find out beforehand (see cybercafé search engines in Chapter 9). Save and back-up your work regularly – accidents will happen and they happen a lot more when equipment is being moved around and support is harder to find. Back-up to a floppy if need be, or a remote site if your office or virtual office (see remote worker resources in Chapter 9) has hard drive space you can use. If not, then remember that you can e-mail your day's work to yourself every evening and it will be safely stored at your e-mail host.

KEY LEARNING POINTS

» Not all jobs are suited for teleworking and not all tasks that can be teleworked should be, so a thorough analysis of the situation is critical.

» Part of that analysis has to be consultation with all involved – ICT department, HR, senior and local management, and the individual workers.

» Managing the attitudes is at least as big a task as maintaining the technology.

» Monitoring success and evaluating performance is an ongoing need.

Frequently Asked Questions (FAQs)

Q1: Is remote and flexible working just another way of saying working from home?

A: No. Home-working is a part of the remote working movement but then so are telecenters, international collaboration, and workers on the move – see Chapter 2.

Q2: Just how much money can a company save?

A: AT&T thinks it has the answer to that one – take a look at adding up the numbers in Chapter 7.

Q3: Does flexible working include productivity on the move?

A: Indeed it does, as demonstrated by the NewsGear project in Chapter 7.

Q4: Does it have benefits for individuals or is it just for the benefit of organizations?

A: Individual benefits are many and valuable – see the second section of Chapter 4 which considers the implications for individual workers.

Q5: How remote is remote?

A: Remote can mean that partners on a project are literally on opposite sides of the planet – see Chapter 5.

Q6: Should all jobs be turned over to teleworking then?

A: No, not all tasks, all jobs, or all workers are suited to teleworking. For a better idea of how and when to make it work, see Chapter 10.

Q7: What kind of companies are profiting from remote working?

A: See Chapter 7 for case studies of different approaches from around the world.

Q8: Telecottaging? Virtual office? Road warrior? What do they all mean?

A: For an explanation of terms and concepts, try Chapter 8 – Key Concepts and Thinkers.

Q9: How is technology going to change telework in the near future?

A: See Chapter 6 – State of the Art.

Q10: Where can I learn more?

A: There is a comprehensive list of further learning resources in Chapter 9.

Acknowledgments

The author gratefully acknowledges the debt owed to Jack Nilles, the father of telecommuting, in the writing of this title.

Index